AS EVER

ALSO BY JOANNE KYGER

AS EVER

SELECTED POEMS

JOANNE KYGER

EDITED WITH A FOREWORD BY MICHAEL ROTHENBERG

INTRODUCTION BY DAVID MELTZER

PENGUIN POETS

PENGUIN BOOKS

Published by the Penguin Group

Penguin Putnam Inc., 375 Hudson Street,
New York, New York 10014, U.S.A.
Penguin Books Ltd, 80 Strand,
London WC2R 0RL, England
Penguin Books Australia Ltd, 250 Camberwell Road, Camberwell,
Victoria 3124, Australia
Penguin Books Canada Ltd, 10 Alcorn Avenue,
Toronto, Ontario, Canada M4V 3B2
Penguin Books India (P) Ltd, 11 Community Centre, Panchsheel Park,
New Delhi – 110 017, India
Penguin Books (N.Z.) Ltd, Cnr Rosedale and Airborne Roads, Albany,
Auckland, New Zealand
Penguin Books (South Africa) (Pty) Ltd, 24 Sturdee Avenue,
Rosebank, Johannesburg 2196, South Africa

Penguin Books Ltd, Registered Offices:
Harmondsworth, Middlesex, England

First published in Penguin Books 2002

Selections on pages 209 to 253 from *Just Space: Poems 1979–1989* by Joanne Kyger. Reprinted
by permission of Black Sparrow Press. Selections from *Going On: Selected Poems 1958–1980*
by Joanne Kyger. Copyright © Joanne Kyger, 1965, 1970, 1975, 1980, 1983. Reprinted by
permission of Dutton, a member of Penguin Putnam Inc. Other selections in this book
appeared in the author's earlier publications, a list of which can be found on page 305.

ISBN 0-14-200112-0
CIP data available.

146119709

To those who love to read

CONTENTS

FOREWORD

In order to hear Joanne Kyger, quiet your mind. Listen carefully. Allow room in your head for the conversation she is having with herself, with others, with you.

Joanne has a truly strong voice—delicate, graceful, and never wasteful. Always lucid. You can hear her speak; her word choice is immaculate.

I have learned more about poetry from Joanne than from any other poet. She is one of the major experimenters, hybridizers, visionaries, and advocates of poetry. But she is too occupied with experience and creation to spend time blowing her own horn. She speaks for poetry first.

Joanne's love for poetry manifests itself in a grander scheme of consciousness-expansion and lesson but is always in the realm of the everyday. Or "just space." She sees all days in every day, where mythologies become the root system. She uses the journal as a hothouse for poetry, where the journal is a place for poems as well as the poem itself.

Joanne does not work to commodify the moment. She writes everywhere, telling a story directly, sequentially, or filtering it as the story itself wants to be told. She's taking it down. Laying out each word, phrase, and space in "projectivity"—an innovator in the "projective line breath." She uses the page for scoring each movement of mind/breath to reflect her experience. Read it out loud. You'll hear her poetry move and pronounce itself, lines shift in speed through space.

Masterful, commanding and quiet, almost transparent, there's life behind the line in Joanne's poetry. It is Joanne herself, listening to the world or "nothing at all," which allows the mind to rest. The poem, poet, and audience—all happens at once.

Space and hesitations. The moment around the hesitation. Then the poignant turn. Joanne's poetry is poetry with attitude. Immediate, playful, colloquial, and instructional. She lets you know where it's at and how to do it and when. Now.

Michael Rothenberg

INTRODUCTION

9:viii:01

Joanne's work and presence have been a part of my life for more than 40 years. We met in North Beach in the late '50s, in the days of Beat vs New Criticism's canon of suck-egg parsons, dons, and tight-assed conservative brilliance, where formalism's top hats were joyously snowballed by speech-based vernacular verse allied to William Carlos Williams. The postwar maelstrom and radioactive pastures opened up the end of traditional Western civilization as all had known and believed in it, and young people were there to pick up the pieces and make new sense of everything and nothing. I was in exile from Brooklyn, brought to the "coast" by my father in search of work. While he stayed in Los Angeles in a no-win decline, his arrogant poet son started hanging out with artists and hipsters and soon defected to San Francisco.

Joanne and her crew (or sangha) were mostly Californians with a very distinct sense of place apart from East Coast folks, especially us New Yorkers whose "wilderness" was Central Park or the Bronx Zoo. It's important to remember (or realize) that those days were before literary academicians freeze-framed them into "movements" or "generations." The slickest, surest way to defang dissent and creative doubt is to accept it and (ugh) incorporate it into glossy narratives circulated throughout institutional castle culture. (A big irony many tapdance around.) Even then, Joanne was a thoughtful and thinking (and self-effacing) poet of deep innate knowing. Her early work was distinctly complex, personal, and resistant to expectations. Her first book, *The Tapestry and The Web*, published in 1965 by the roshi of New American Poetry, Donald M. Allen, displayed a complex yet playful reflection of her apprenticeship years in the North Beach academy of bars and pads and galleries under the generous and cranky pedagogy of Jack Spicer and Robert Duncan.

Her work demands and awakens attention to the extraordinary ordinary, the so-called "everyday"; daybook moments written by a highly selective eye/I selectively and attentively annotating what's before and beyond her eyes.

10:viii:01

Like her ally and mentor Philip Whalen, Kyger is an unorthodox American Buddhist. Heterodoxical yet profoundly traditional to the essence of the practice, deeply devoted to her own earned terms of spirit and self-awareness. Practice does not make perfect, nor do I believe perfection is the goal; her poetry consistently illustrates perfection imma-nent in the everyday.

Joanne's work slides in and out of range as an aside, a quip, a flip so-and-so that turns inside out and you're face to face in emptied space, smashed ego scattered all over the place, beyond repair, within transformation. Her casual familiar gossipy tone, sometimes flustered and always self-critical, disarms and alarms us in the brilliance of what's re-vealed. Nothing's hidden or concealed from her attention. If there's a secret, it's any-where, everywhere.

11:viii:01

An ongoing poetics of place and realization of self therein. Kyger's hometown commu-niqués are an informal epic, less arcane and self-conscious than *Paterson* or the *Maximus Poems*. How a life is lived with wonder and drudgery, devotion, and a reckless certainty at home in the absolute core of nothing and everything in a moment. No other poet of my generation has been able to make the pleasures and particulars of the "everyday" as luminous and essential and central.

Early influences were the grand mind lights of Robert Duncan and Jack Spicer, and no doubt William Carlos Williams. But the bridge is Philip Whalen, whose "mind graphs" allow, as they demonstrate, an expansive and nonauthoritarian attempt to write a dis-tinctive yet unofficial poetry. Meditations that track the streams and strands of mind in its continuum and flight from captivity.

12:viii:01

We're all in the living room—Joanne, Tina, Arthur Okamura—singing in sincere neo-barbershop exuberance: "Sentimental Journey."

13:viii:01

the shed on her property (then), rough but intensely comfortable with comforters, candles, and fresh-cut flowers in a precious vase no different than those chianti bottles beatniks stuck their candles into.

14:viii:01

going over the twisty hills into San Francisco to a poetry reading; Joanne raving apologetically about Jane Austen.

15:viii:01

never much talk of Zen, as if it weren't yet as evident everywhere.

poems replete with graceful attention and an almost courteous relation to the world and reader.

poems astute with hard tact.

poems unknowable in the knowing.

16:viii:01

rowdy dances in town; loud late-night celebrating. Trancing back home with immensely present thick soup of stars overhead and tame and wild dogs barking on the mesa. Their turn.

Joanne's garden through the decades.

Reggae tapes out of the boom box through open doors.

5:ix:01

fluttery fluting like Billie Burke, enwrapped in layers of scarves of varied patterns; rings, bracelets, breathless, alert, off to the lagoon to watch egrets stand still in the water.

7:ix:01

dancing all night long to Smiley's jukebox Saturday night blow-out

8:ix:01

letters, manuscripts, papers, stored and stacked in boxes on a shelf covered with a madras curtain.

everything considered in its place, there for a reason. Bowl of fruit on kitchen table; one-of-a-kind bowl from Japan filled with pine nuts; round brass trivet from India whose heart is a brass lotus; Buddhas, all sizes, on shelves hidden and revealed, everything in its moment suddenly seen.

9:ix:01

paintings by Nemi Frost, Tom Field, Arthur Okamura.

candle glowing caves of incense and drapes as out of the Arabian Nights fantasy. Miles Davis—"Bye Bye Blackbird"—on the hi-fi.

10:ix:01

drinking singing dancing

pass the pipe

late into night

next to the ocean

selah

David Meltzer

AS EVER

THE MAZE

I saw the
dead bird on the sidewalk
his neck uncovered
and prehistoric

At seven in the morning
 my hair was bound
 against the fish in the air
 who begged for the ocean
 I longed for their place

Behind the
 tall thin muslin of the curtain
 we could see his shadow
 knocking
 and we waited
 not stirring
 crouched by the fireplace
   where the ashes blew out

 later we checked the harbor
 to see if it was safe
   rather hoping
   one had gone astray
   and flung itself upon the shore
    for all to watch

If I should weep
 they would never know

 and so I walked
 silently
 shrugging off hands
 in treacherous places
   wanting to fall

In Williamsburg, Virginia

my uncle
pointed out the Maze
which grew
in the dead
            governor's garden

delighted

I went to it

and stood
poised
inside the
precise
entrance

like a long hallway
the tightly trimmed
bushes
held themselves
pointing each
leaf
and twig
in an unquestioning manner

white gravel
caressed my feet

the sky disappeared
and I
could hear
the sound of water
rushing

I knew each corner
without pausing

Held captive in a cave
Ulysses
sobbed for his wife
who was singing high

melodies
from the center of a
cobweb shawl
of their design

three feathers
I picked
from a stone
in my path

and turning at last
I saw
the speckled bench
and halting fountain
which marked
the end.

       She

tortures
    the curtains of the window
        shreds them
        like some
              insane insect

creates a
        demented web
    from the thin folds
    her possessed fingers
    clawing   she
thrusts them away with
sharp jabs   of long pins
             to the walls.

1958

TAPESTRY

The anticipation of one
grey hound
his front
legs raised

The faces of
five huntsmen
show
the legend

A million leaves
and flowers
placed into
life   they

are urgent.

And to drink I
must bow
down
before you

small birds   they
taste of your life

they
know
they
know
and

quickly

music sounds on my
ear

brush the
green oak and

holly
heron and
peach tree
caught

    The mother has
    blest us   and I

    am surrounded
    by the life
    not of this
    story

        6.58

THE DANCE

a step into
the dance
this
progression towards
creation

the Ceylonese Bodhisattva
                    12 centuries old

seated
        one heel out
leans
        thighs bent
as if he will
enter into the dance

an excitement
from the position of his body
we make one movement / repeat it

he is poised as if to make
the new one

wrist bent out
three fingers touch
the palm of this hand
        Body sleek

and wet as if rising from the river

assured
the rising
the step
is his
when he pleases.

TAPESTRY

                              the eye

                           is drawn

                        to the Bold

               DESIGN —— the

                      .Border.

                    .California flowers.

nothing promised that   isn't shown.

                           Implements:

                        shell

                        stone

                    .Peacock.

Somewhere you can find reference to the fact that PAN was the

son of PENELOPE

Either as the result of a *god*

or as a result of ALL of the suitors

who hung around while Odysseus was abroad.

12.29 & 30 (Pan as the Son of Penelope)

Refresh my thoughts of Penelope again.

Just HOW
     solitary was her wait?

I notice Someone got to her that

       barrel chested he-goat prancing
       around w/ his reed pipes

is no fantasy of small talk.
More the result of BIG talk
       and the absence of her husband.

And what a cockeyed lecherous offspring. What a birth
       THAT must have been. Did she turn away & sigh?

I believe she dreamed too much. Falling into her weaving,

       creating herself as a fold in her tapestry.

      a flat dimension character of beauty
     keeping one task in mind and letting nothing *Human* touch her
—which is pretend.

     She knew what she was doing.

       OUTSIDE
     of that he grabbed her.

     Some thing keeps escaping me.   Something

   about the landing of the husband's boat upon the shore.

She did not run up and embrace him as I recall.

     He came upon her at the house & killed the suitors.

I choose to think of her waiting for him
                concocting his adventures   bringing
        the misfortunes to him
—she must have had her hands full.

And where did she hide her impudent monster?

He was acres away by then I suppose in the sunlight leching
                at some round breasted sheep

girl.

    the cock crowing at dawn never had bigger thoughts than he did

  about waking up the world.

A song in the rope   taut against the wind
A song in the wire   taut against the wind

       Needless to say this could have been his very course
  He *did*
travel far away
      from where she waited

    But bitches there are
   even at sea—although that one takes a bit more
tender handling, it's still all bluff
     a matter of riding out the storm.

       Now wind is another matter
    that is who he had to close his ears to

and worse at night the sound, I am You, I am You, Join.

    and what does it touch which is deep
    and are men willingly driven over rails

      a scream higher than a woman's
    at any forbidden place.

I am watching what is happening now
it seems that water is being pushed from both sides of the boat
as we make our passage thru it.
We don't have to stop

and can hardly blame our follies to the breeze.

                  FEBRUARY 1960
                  Somewhere in the Pacific

waiting again
what for

I am no picker from the sea of its riches
I watch the weaving—the woman who sits at her loom
What was her name? the goddess I mean
—not that mortal one

plucking threads
as if they were strings of a harp

SPRING, 1960
Kyoto

They are constructing a craft
    solely of wood
at Waka-no-ura, fishing village,
    a jewel quite naturally
from the blue of the farm house tile roofs.

      found on the southern coast.

The women pull by hand long strings
      of seaweed across the shore

it dries

        At the other end of the town
      the hull of the boat rises
above the smaller houses
A little prince of a boy in a white knit suit
    stands with the others in a group on the beach

Watching us go by, we are strange.

      The women bend over
the seaweed, wakame, changing its face to the sun.

It is lonely

I must draw water from the well   75 buckets for the bath

I mix a drink—gin, fizz water, lemon juice, a spoonful
                                        of strawberry jam

And place it in a champagne glass—it is hard work
            to make the bath

And my winter clothes are dusty and should be put away

In storage. Have I lost all values I wonder
            the world is slippery to hold on to

When you begin to deny it.

Outside outside are the crickets and frogs in the rice fields

Large black butterflies like birds.

outside where the storm goes cracked
he says you cant come in
hold the baby under your saree
and I'm going to sit up here and watch you
in this purple velvet lined tower of
mine,   and look at the fruit tree
and watch all the red and yellow pears and
cheeries jiggle when it lightnings and
after while maybe I'll have
the chokidar bring up some tea and a plum
and a whole bunch of candy and stuff
and you'd just better stay down there
and get all crummy and muddy.

CAPTION FOR A MINIATURE

1962
New Delhi

MY SISTER EVELYNE

Sarnath
Tuesday, February 13
        near the evening, 5:05

        the child with his temper tantrum
        this morning on the deer park path
            his white satin dress
    rolling
on the red ground.   Evelyne
            every morning in Illinois
        screeching
                on the kitchen floor
                    before breakfast exhausting
            us all, she also cried
        when we gave her a new rubber doll
            in despair
            her glasses fastened around her head
    with a wide rubber band
                black eyes crossed
        in rage.
                all of us waiting for gratitude

    She had a plaid dress
that we took her to school in. She was sent home
    too young. In her harness and green snow
        suit straining, pink cheeks
        chapped. The father
    stands holding her back from the snow.

            At 8 she sat in the carved high backed
    chinese chair
        quietly, Nancy thought she was ill
        at my 14th birthday party

17

Louise is her middle name
a foul tongued determination
brought material rewards for her
an extra piece of meat, TV dinners served
in the dark, expensive shoes.
perfect teeth

TAPESTRY

Dealing with the detail
on the fragment of the fifth
Tapestry the maid whose head
is turned sideways her eyes
shifted upwards in what
seems
coquettish towards
the sound of the
huntsman's horn the
capture
then of the
unicorn. Her hair is uncombed.
and hand
raised up in a lackadaisical gesture
meaning all's well.

You can tell.
Puffeyes and the broken turned nose.
Searching
for bigger & better things.

4.62
Kyoto

BURNING THE BABY TO
MAKE HIM REALER

Dipping him at night in the kitchen
    the rest are asleep
by one hand into the flames
      just out of a desire of niceness
The lady of the earth wandering
        in sorrow
tries to give him a gift but he screams
      & the mother awakes rushing into the room

And where is my daughter, where is she
I'll teach you all a lesson
you'll never forget

      Gary says of the blond child
    tensely crouching on the porch he's
  not human.   at 2½ an unfaltering
icy blue stare in his eyes he DEMANDS
    Both hands before him, uh-uh,
  want, want
     & his parents cower
      what is it, what is it you want.
a wake of smashed cookies, crushed lipstick wet cigarettes
    & nervous haste, no joy
      ripping the morning glories 3 times from the pot

ILIAD: ACHILLES DOES NOT DIE

Leaving him alive abruptly that way
& the burial & the keening
for the other at the end of the dry plain
the stream burned alive
the wave crashing down dies
mid-way

12 men sacrificed for Patrocles

How big was the distance of Troy
& the battlefield, the shoreline
of ships—does it stretch as far
as the city of Kyoto

& no more of Helen
who takes her back?   soft as
a throw of silk
& she said, perhaps
I dreamed it all.

the length & breadth
of all that chasing

& Helen still quiet at home
tending to the needs of the household—

how Homer dislikes Paris

& here is Achilles stript stript   left.
waits, but the story ends
this blanket of air
& the tenderness of mortals.

fragmented.   ie

several valleys.

Unfortunately unable to give you the plain D. can present of
    wheat, corn etc.   only bravado on my part
to hope to be blessed with complete vision.   I'm sure
    you can see me better
than I can.
        Dealing with one sided particulars, loneliness
    contempt & godliness,
            Play is occasional
        scrambling around by accident.

            We took the left fork
up into Yase valley at the rise of the hill, used only
        by woodsmen, charcoal makers.
                    moving farther
and farther back into the valley burning trees as they go
        Situated on near inaccessible
    hillsides and their families, smoking out the wood.
                    Way up on top
where you'd like to think he was a poet hermit
        grunting in the cold, fixing up his charcoal,
                    not reveling
        in any city way about nature
    maybe he's mean.   all their abandoned junk
                from house to house.
            The greased log rails
    for pulling lumber,
12 inches apart or so, on my hands and knees.

            packing all the lacquer boxes
    with mild tasting flavors, off to Ninaji
            cutting off the new back highway

with yellow dirt exposed like the west
& the last of the 200 shrines   all dusty now & the windows torn
for the famous double nosed cherries.

5,000 cups of sake later
talent abounds & the leaves pulled off the tree.

She dances
She dances
gravely.

this way
& that,   an arm
or a fan
for her face,   and her feet
hardly turn

Picking up & using
everything, the gravel
on the river bed
and the river moves on
that's what it is.
and the water changes too, hardly the same drop
gets through.   that's all we can hope for

2.63

Look the bird is making plans
talking to men in the room upstairs
poking at crumbs in the kitchen
using *our* toilet
& whose rights do I worry about
Keep the house
I'll
go bird you keep this place
at the very farthest wall
pushing & scratching to get out
thru the cracks in the batten
where the light comes in after storms
& the weeds tear thru in August
all all
has fled
has gone flicked by
& scratched the soil.
& you claw foot   fix it
fix it   I'm going.

4.63

24

THE HUNT IN THE WOOD:
PAOLO UCCELLO

The greyhounds go leaping into the woods
    the hunters behind them
and the trees have their lower branches cut
      So the men with their poles will not be struck
        and a horse has suddenly stopped
      on a ring of flowers the rider crying Ho
        up to the sky
    Small figures way
back in the woods with the hounds shout
    The white hounds this way and that
   like bounding deer or rabbits
      And the deer
here he is with the antlers,   by the pond
       closed in upon
    They move from the dark of the wood
to the midst, the racing men and their ribbons
   and the deer rushes back towards them.

My father died this spring
        Well, I had meant to write more often
To a kind of hell it must be, with all unresolved difficulties.
      I had greens with vinegar last night—that's something
in common
        And I would have told him that—adding it
     to a list of possible conversations
With the pictures on his dressing table
     of all his daughters
but he wasn't flinging out his arms to keep a soul there.
         You can't say he wasn't strange
  and difficult.
       How far does one go
  to help a parent like a child—when he waits
    at the employees entrance in old clothes
     and I don't want him.
         Well he'll be there waiting
for me. Demands just, wanted, or not
    are to be met.
And let me see, yes the demon large
    impossible and yields without vanishing
  no power, no satisfaction
     sitting on the back porch drinking beer
    following me to the sick squirrels in the cellar.
And the material things, calling cards
   engraved watches, trunks that married life brings
    full of stuff
he left behind 10 years ago. The golf clubs. The fact is
   there was a man, a married man,
   and an old man. it's impossible to know.
    but blood does bring curiosity.

9.15.63
Kyoto

26

THOSE THINGS WE SEE ARE
IMAGES OF THE PAST

From now, always, on the turning point, viewing back
              and that delicious interpretation
    is the world, HOW CLEVER OF US

              An entirely new thing each time
        blind or not about it, always inventive—seeing
        stones,
    persimmons,
moving a stone in dirt, oh where does it go
        she's fleet footed
    to be a tree, to be Jack Spicer in a dream
        to carry this around all day.   and every night
    the waves chuck full of things to happen

                    As clear as you can See
        it's done, isn't it, isn't that a *fact*.

        Right to the water's edge
        That's a wall.
    Do you talk to each other well?

    I miss each time. up she went her arms went into willow
        And do *you* feel
        what you put down is fine, precious.

The persimmons are falling
early and rotten from the tree.
                    no time to attend the garden.
     where I go like a dandy
  is to the living room
             and right to the heart of the matter.

•

From here   to here.
    how much are you going to do.
               It occurred to me yesterday
people don't die at thirty.
          But the bloom is gone.   all this
    awareness of a bloom to die.   what a sad time
when the point is clear and we settle down like ripe wheat
       the beginning business over.

•

There reoccurs a dream
of a large mysterious house, of women in turbans
     gigantic attics of rubbish
a long staircase, mysterious inhabitors
   of closed off suites, marble fountains,
      sneaking through the house
in by the back way, I can't take over.

The great house has strange furniture I'm unfamiliar with.
    In a chair in the living room
I don't know a thing, about what's around the corner.
going up the staircase, knocking on the doors.

The different preoccupations. years and years
go by. A bad crop of persimmons eaten with bugs
this year, a good one last. And the wrinkles.
                    Melting into the nice earth
giving over life, giving it another child.

•

'You've built this vast house, now explore it.'
—Some people have well lived rooms.

DECEMBER 1963

WAITING

over the lilacs won't he   come home

to at least rest tonight,   I want to see

the round car safe in the driveway, cinders

and the moon over head

THE ODYSSEY POEMS

'Where ever you go I am with you.'
                    and bring you back.

———————————————————

            The morning venus
        sailing into the bay,
                    lifting them asleep onto the land
            he has returned to
        and doesn't know where he is.
                    outside of San Francisco
                        the long paths and eucalyptus
                            are another country

                                Oh he is a liar
                    from the bottom of his heart
            But he puts facts together
        and has,   little rival, and lets no one know.

            The real earth
        moves and falls away into pieces in the north.
He comes back, was he led astray,   the land has abundance
                    corn and wine, rain
            springs, the forest

                    wild fields of flowers take him out
        with your own eyes you make sure
        ———————————————————

                        there are disguises

        the way he dresses
    in old clothes and moves like an old man
            no one knows the real facts
                all the goods he carries and where

can he put them, stow it away, his property
taking it into the mountains
                    leaving the fine things at home
          going into the house
     where everything is put in place, set into movement

               Oh I have
set eyes on you again, that I should—

     the gold, the perfect copper and fine cloth

     and set it apart just like stone
          2 guarding the entrance to Ithaca

                                                  II

          Whether he is dead or not and that animal moves up the hall
     I am mortal.
     ————————————————————

                    The old man, the pig herder, who
          like Andy says, tell me what it is,
          let me take care of you
     The swineherd in charge of the pigs
          his oak stockade
made from the heart of the tree
                    three hundred and sixty
          of them to herd.
               'I never go to town except for news.'
                    keeping the dogs off strangers.   'See I know
                         you are hogs
watching the others back in the grove, moving them
          They are feeding on acorns they love and drinking water.'

     'When I returned a second time here there was an evening sun
                    and I swam ashore
     and crouched in the thickets'

offered a fine meal.
Take away part of this animal, the ridge of hair, throw it in the fire
and the throat is slit, singe the bristles, cut it up.

She is
goddess of the dawn, her vehicle, the wild boar, stands on him
as a handsome animal.

It moves
outside it is being done
the brightest of all stars

and w/ bristles raised the hogs can run
thru the grove, the ground swept bare, like a kitchen floor would be

He wraps his cloak

and goes out

to watch those pigs

under a rock from the wind.

4.9.64

III

Land at the first point you meet

He wonders   whether he will be caught or get through alive
and in the morning tells them all he's leaving.
I see this star up there, thru the white sides of the house, the night is over.

Helen rises

He is given a fine meal to start on his journey
the fire is laid, wood split, meat roasted

and Helen gives him a great robe, embroidered by herself.

      At sea bodies are thrown over
seals and porpoise follow the boat.
            Birds day after day that never rest picking up garbage.

    See there is an eagle that ate a goose

        He leaves the ship, walking at a good pace

    directly to the house of his friend.

4.15.64

Still after 15 years or more she doesn't know
and may go off with the likeliest and most generous suitor

The best of the lot comes from the corn and grass lands,
wise, and she gives him approval
But what's on her mind?

She never refuses or accepts
stands against a pillar of the house,
watching and planning.

Well the men,
they give a lot of insults to anyone that comes by,
wine running,
dancing with the maids, 112 people
eating every day

She comes and rages
quit eating the coffee cake and cottage cheese
put the lid on the peanut butter jar
sandwiches made of cucumber, stop eating the *food!*

climbing over the rough ravine
and up an impossible cliff, naked, you mark how high you can go
coming back to his opinion of her or hers of him
listening sometimes
to *him* raging, you leave me alone.   you dream of me.
and there, she withdrew

and wept for odysseus
until, what bird is it?   that swoops in definite circles in the sky
comes down and puts her to sleep

for by day my one relief is to weep and sigh

                             Am I to stay

      winding and coming back, goes out and sees, dreams

are awkward things

             a cigarette falls behind the bed

                        I *can't* get out of bed

                                she pushes

        where where are the walls,

     out the window the poetry, dishes broken, things torn up, please

         please don't weep anymore.

               the suitors are sickened w/ blood, look

        how they decay, kill them all

      an eagle takes a terrified dove

and she places a good chair to hear what goes on

Here it is, the last day.   and what has happened.
    Penelope had at least one night with her husband.
      And he'll have to go on again to find another city

    without salt and away from the sea.
      She takes this as a matter of course. It is interesting to note

how cautious she was, he called her iron hearted, to see if it was really
      he that had returned

    until she went to bed. It's good to be clear about what you do.
    They had a party. The pigman and cowherd, also the son
    drank wine and danced. This was after the killing.
      Not a new marriage as some might have thought
12 ladies were hung by the neck.
    as usual Penelope slept through all this.

        I think she is happy now.
    her household is restored.
and she knows he will die an old and comfortable death.
up to your room now to wait a while he tells her
    and she does what he says.
      I guess it's good to know where you're going.

MAY 22, 1964

＊＊＊

there is no meeting
and they could not string the bow
            Memory has no direction,
        a soft weeping like rain drumming dry soil

            give me a pile of grape leaves
            give me a lot of wine

Geraniums

Taking a walk in the morning
the warm mist like rain

Jack picked a nasturtium about 7

Quiet lake with water lilies
no one harms anything that comes down there

the family comes with smiles

thru the large luxurious rooms of the house

scattered thru in white clothing like flowers
take your time, take your time

this is a guest house where all are taken care of
the great and good sun comes out, the sun is a star

She finished up the web, it had to do with her father she said
using it to keep them away for many years, tricking them.
Hermes came to get the dead suitors.

Persephone really died every year
to go down there was difficult a large dark house
and ghost groves on either side one of white.   They called her terrible

It has been difficult to write this.   One day
I walked around the block, it was grey, and whatever was green on the lawns was clear
the flower pots on the back porch, the neighbor's steps to the second floor
I could have watched for a long time,

why they must go to war I can't decide

to settle fear.   we were all born
They are coming towards the house someone calls to Odysseus
and he is that great fighter
having a guide, a female presence who pulls her own self into battle also
A great struggle in Persephone's field of poppies
a broken sprig of geranium
It is not for me to control she calls
the loud men rising towards each other, great turmoils that pull
through all of you,   I give you style in battle
the final control is man
Zeus calls halt.
takes all this nature from running riot, the thundering push
of green buds, leaves, grass, roaring
in the sky filling it with birds, the clouds
closing down, mountains rocking, sinks

a flaming bolt,   the control takes peace

over an ordered landscape, it is clear
all confusion gone, and nodding their heads wondered where they had gone.

12.1.64

THE PIGS FOR CIRCE IN MAY

I almost ruined the stew and Where
is my peanut butter sandwich I tore through the back of the car
I could not believe
there was One slice of my favorite brown bread and my stomach and
I jammed the tin foil and bread wrappers into the stew
and no cheese and I simply could not believe
and you Never
TALK when my friends are over.

This is known as camping in Yosemite.

Already I wish there was something done.
Odysseus found a stag on his way to the ship
I think of people *sighing* over poetry, *using* it,   I
don't know what it's for. Well,

Hermes forewarned him.   Can you imagine
those lovely beasts all tame   prancing around him?

She made a lot of pigs too.

I like pigs.   Cute feet, cute nose,   and I think

some spiritual value investing them. A man and his pig together,
rebalancing the pure in them, under each other's arms, bathing,
eating it.

And when the time came, she did right
Let them go
They couldn't see her when she came back
from the ship, seating themselves and wept, the wind
took them directly north, all day
into the dark.
at least they were moving again

Sometimes I just go hobbling up and say
Just a little *Food*, please. Usually a piece of bacon or toast

the coffee curling up in the pine groves of Yosemite. There is a rock wall
in the night.
animals and something hot and dank on the sand trail in the sun,
waste.

Odysseus went down and got his comrades
'Circe says its ok to stay.' And they were freely bathed and wined.
She had a lot of maids and a staid housekeeper.
I mean I admire her. The white robes
and keeping busy
She fed her animals

wild acorns, and men crying inside

with a voice like a woman
from the sun and the ocean
She is busy at the center, planning out great
stories to amuse herself, and a lot of pets,
a neat household, gracious
honey and wine
She offers.
Purple linen on the chairs
Odysseus mopes
'Oh I'll give you your bores back' They weep to see each other
a black ram
and a young ewe and the ship to hell
where persephone has left only one man with reason
She doesn't hold them back
a young man dies
that is his fault.

And she asked him to stay
climbing all day
pushing

strewn with boulders
                    the great leap it makes
into space, giddy, he rushes at her
          the roar he makes
                    on the wide shelf bed
     they both watch over the edge

          and the Great Pigs waddle off in the sky—

She comes up
a long walk behind her

and all the struggle of what will happen today.
The dirt laying limply
over everything
and the laundry has been soaking for two days in the bathroom sink.
I am so worried.

the angry wife screeching in the kitchen

When persephone comes back in spring
there is a party
Beneath there is melancholy
and the ghosts of the house are laid to rest.
This is my house.
creaking and rushing through the house the others go mad
I have to mop the floors again.

She is taken
swiftly away.
The pigs of the crevice
are filled again.

'I thought there had been a great war.
Did you make me a promise? I gave a great groan
from the lungs and the stomach
bellowing to be free.'

I didn't want to think
about what to say. How many people can hear my natural relatives
die anyway the rain was coming down. Outside it's like clear air
whistling around you and eat flesh.

"A climate of order in which lawful governments can function
effectively."

to keep it clean

from bar to bar
her yellow eyes

     one does not get enough

Even in the rain the wall
is a molecule of me? when I die

     the mind takes space, *whose* control?

               the war in Viet-nam

   is there. it is speaking to you I wish to say

How long is it we stay together.

                          11.12.65

From THE IMAGINARY APPARITIONS

The center of the garden

well it was the garden itself, sitting

in the middle, the walks leading to it from either side,
the paths stop short of the center of the garden
you go through the trees

You appear in the center of the garden
you can see them walking there now. The road
is not so troubled. There are accidents by the path
but they walk on untroubled feet
the wolf devouring the pig
and when they lay cradled, the feet sleeping
crablike, they were walking here

and they were walking there.

⸺ ⸻ ⸺

Like a lantern
it was interesting to find structure in that mess. The tall men
riding the light. A deeper forest, they came from,
but the grass at their feet was children's grass, from
regular statements, from zigzag lines.
They rise
taking their way, the struggle of heads, walking
strong and oblivious, with pomp and rich robes saying
we are the minds of this country.

I didn't know which direction.
                    She whispers
in his ear. And he listens like one big eye.
                              More important
          in the park, a dainty animal
      like a monkey, strolls. She is large and hen-like
                  He is glassy eyed from listening
          his nose is stopped up
                    She kisses his ear
          it is taking its time
clear and fragile in the park, like an idea of his
                  and above it

      like a dark red bruise, the house.

AUGUST 18
for Jack Spicer

      They said the moon wasn't going to rise no no
where will it come up so we can see what's happening
                  in the night
            the light sharply behind us.
                    I saw him like a shadow rise

      far above us, in the night
where the stars were, and he said, wait.
                    I can't wait.

Like stickle burrs the moon attacks us. The old things
closing around us. Everyone alone, groaning,
and the ring of light around the moon,

was there, it was hanging

I never finished, I lied, and through me

it came bursting

I never finished, and all alone
                        close to the moon
on the top of a hill or a piece of land
        burr-like he closes over us.

⸎

                              In the high

            clear air

                                        it was icy

            Did you Feel good?

    I rose, I rose

                                    above you all

            Did you worry

48

               how it could go
            together? the one presses
         against the other, and the trees cling
   and the trees grow and the mountain

                                                    rises

                                          the sky

                   changes around the sky

      changes.

                         —⊶   ⊶⊰⊱⊷   ⊷—

                            There are acres and acres of fields to go,
   I won't look for a light note, as it rushes past under us,
            the meeting of two lopsided people, his eyes are
         sad, she has none, their hands meet. Under the soil
   all that twisting and turning, she suckles his breast
                  and between them another rises, the child
            whom she kisses. And he looks solidly forward
         and a tiny light breaks for her eye. The grand scarlet sunset

   is above them and they are like fish in the field. I would break
   the network from that house behind them, as he beckons,
   and like she is pummeling down from the sun,
   she bows her head to kiss him.

                                  49

PLACES TO GO

I–VI & HERE

I

Perhaps you can remember this all if you think hard enough.
It was a country where the summers were always warm clear into
the late evening and at eleven or so a comforting breeze came
up and into the windows and over the bedsheets. Sometimes
there was rain and thunder and the sighing of tree branches when
the rain got them.

Can you imagine? The night was just as comfortable as the
day. She would go down to the lake during the day, the long
road down the bluff, and swim. About a half mile down the
shore there were cliffs all oozing with clay and animals who
lived in holes there.

There was a pier to swim off, made of white cement. She would
take her sister to the lake on the bike, now sometimes it was
hard, the road wobbled and turned to mud. Also a few other
difficulties like saying "Damn" which was completely draining.
There were pebbles on the floor of the lake and these could have
been simply carted away but they weren't. The faces shimmer
on the beach, it is impossible to know who they are,
I mean one never does *know*.

One of the worst was when the Oz book got lost. It was under
the cushion on the couch, but it meant stealing at least 75
cents or maybe 17 and getting to the mail first.

Part of the difficulty of walking down the pier was falling
off, it would tilt and sway and suddenly be covered with water
and even if you were driving an automobile down it the water
might come up and run across the wheels and lord, there wasn't
a place to be safe in.

       A better thing was floating or flying.
First it is a matter of taking off the wooden lifesaver and

the water holds you without it. Flying, sometimes you cannot
rise far enough above the ground, or when you are chased, fast
enough and sometimes so natural and comfortable and smiling
you can do your little flight.

Of course the winds come while the sister does ballet, open-
ing the bags of wind on the deck, letting them loose they
blow and blow the ship, and she was younger, younger than any
of them.

When they found her covered in mud half up to her neck, struggling
with the wind. Well, falling on the ice. It was a game, cutting
the knee, brushing the leaves it is time to point out dogtooth
violets. This is the way babies are born, they come with the
first snow, and everyone knows, like the taste of snow and women
under the mattress ships rise and sink.

                I know this girl and she said
she was on a mountain once and could put her tongue right on
a cloud, it was fuzzy. I wish she was right. There was also
the matter of a store on the fence and tomato *slices* just left
on the posts, the flies buzzing, well, it was a bit exciting.

When they get worried and padded, get everything in sight, the
handle comes off the carpet sweeper. Blood in the toilet, murder
takes the arms and legs and head, like a cat walking high
above, stealing.

How did I get this way, who stole in. Covered with shit, you
have still taken me away, the eyes on the lawn, the endless
meals, the wrong kind of doll, she's not *pretty*.

The large large house with their dogs, a lonely one by the
lake, finally to get there, leader, and the heart simply lifts,
the loud voice not too loud now, shining, truly shining, walking up
the long hill in the sun.

This is the ghost one I was referring to.

II

My place was losing the
great beauty that came on horse reaching out to me as I lay
locked, no I won't and running after, I want I want. Nearly
falling like a ghost, telling it like a ghost, becoming wet.
Waiting.

I'll take it out again, the asking for candy and sweet in
the woods where they go. I know of course, and can't get
through, just skating on thin ice out of danger bringing them
candy and sweet away from the toes, being caught.

So then there seemed to be many things. She almost caught
me, as I looked up and was falling or I was looking down and
was falling. This was there worry.

I didn't know how far
it could extend, where ever the first move is to be made.

They hammer on the trees in the woods those boys, wearing
white shirts, and guns.

III

Now it sours. The things I made, I guess, are all a result,
held away, the latter portion blooms.

Evelyne watched all
the way through, the medium, rattling around, how, was it being
sized up, when it is being left, unattended.

I can see now
why I cut it away and called it my own. They were cut away, the
whole world blooms. I cut the dead branch off the honeysuckle,
it started out last June going halfway up the porch.

It is better now the dead portion is cut away. It is still
true that I can fold, I mean the room can tilt, but half and
half, that's how it blooms.

I don't know it exactly, but he was struck blind when women
had pleasure the most that they did not want to hear; or saw
wrongly. Was he born one way and then the other. But he knew
both as a man, lay dying, along the stream of blood to talk.

One side sleeps, the other awakes. I would not worry of dream,
if I were you. It does not lurk, Saying it now, if you care to
remember, oh, Did I say that?

Nobody knows what they want. They
can plan it out and get that beautiful construction, I mean
mine is the most beautiful but I never get what I want. You
can't put the rocks in your *mouth* on the seashore, rub them
in your eyes.

IV

When my Daddy said it was Christmas he brought us a first aid
kit from the Drug Store for Evelyne and did Mother get bath-
salts, a flashlight? The night before Christmas, whatever
did he give me. At least my Mother would say, on Christmas
morning, This is from your Father, and this is from your Father
and me, etc. And he would never know, except the year he burned
the war bonds in the wrapping paper in the morning.

Well

in the war I dreamed he died, it is never right, Under the
Lilacs I wept for him to return. Carrying on with the
woman in Chicago, I Know he's got a woman up there

                                        It's not

beaten or gotten through.

                    He went to the concerts at Christmas
though, the choir and the orchestra. Let's see history, let's
get down to the hard facts. War of 1812 and Pocahontas. I
can't go there,

it is the cut away part, unattended, sitting on the chair on
the porch who can remember the most. At Christmas they are
up all night, can they get everything ready in time, they are
like lumbering Southern ghosts, when the sun rises and sets
on Daddy.

V

                    Came up on a horse. Those
days were like breaking through sunlight, where the sand would
bite at the feet. God is with you. I do poems before I go
to sleep, these are dream poems, there is Snow White's bottom.

How high are the fences around? There are still areas to
play in, washing hair, poor Joanne. Margaret took her first
bite by herself.

And the terrible boredom, waiting, in the sun, with a house
folded of cardboard and crayon people against the walls. Carrots,
the girl next door, and we ate them.

                    Also the stone road goes
down perilously, the same pier awash, the water slide into the
deep depths.

VI

The earth was cracking open, earthquakes. The earth was end-
ing, if you read the newspaper, the comet sped across the sky,
like neon lights of constellations.

What did you say, poetry
was bad and for the gutter?

How did you say that? How was I going from side to side. It
is possible to see, spending everything the wrong way. How
did you happen to get here and see the cathedrals and did you
see a picture before? Again, gazing at her feet the earth
opened up. Tall buildings shaking oh yes one can wait it
out in the country, well I never thought to move at that moment,
it's just the way it was. Figuring out what other people see
I'm going to have to sing this song very rapidly, I can't say it
quite so fast, my voice cracks.

HERE

It is very easy to listen to when they spell it out easy.
I would listen to my grandmother, or was it my aunt. Give
it back to me my mother said to my grandmother, it is mine,
you gave it to me. It was a book on child raising. I thought
my grandmother was going to read it to us. I step
on snails. A red setter came into the kitchen and ate half
the turkey in the oven. Before I got locked up. I shit in
a pail. Take out the clothespins first. The cat did similarly
just like it was born to, on newspapers in the garage. After
that I went into training, developing artistic talents.

Can you act my mother said, and she whapped me on the
knuckles with the dinner knife. Out there again

doing the same things with newspaper and it flees from me.
I tried, I tried, I *am* good, anything, as quick as a wink.
Santa Claus came in the bathroom window. Where did they
all go to. It isn't any good remembering, every inch of
energy for getting home and candy store. I know you are
taking things and I threw them in the canal.

                                        They need it
I wish I wasn't so much older. Like the parrot in the cage
knowing what to listen to. It scatters away sparkling and
shaking, rising like the canals they fish dead children out of,
rising the water across your feet. It's simple to know,
I guess you should use the toilet. It's not fun, the trees shake
the sky races, watch me watch me, sparkling and
sprinkling and shaking.

Dear, Dearest

alone in this room, the steampipes hiss. I have three windows
Two look out on a wall, but it is white.

                              Brought before
the lady Anne he is white, he raises his tiny hoof
He is Christ

                    To break the chain of events
                    I am not certain
unless you move towards me, that you want what you ask for.
                              I saved for you so long
when I did not care well for myself
                    crumpled and torn
          rising from a fast embrace always
     signed with my name
                    or is it
you cannot help yourself
          and he kneels down
                         though the blood may pass freely
          as to when murdered
     When it is cold, and a cold sun
   has been waiting all day
and the coleus got nipped in the frost, barely
     hardly remember what you say, like keep together
          kept the blood flowing, where we can barely find them like
               in some dreamland
          they all speak words of love to each other.

                              1.66
                              for John Wieners

A NOVEL

CHAPTER ONE

I woke up very angry because I wanted to see where they
were and I couldn't see where they were.

I thought get it over with, spewing great foul smells
into the air confused as to what could join and what could not.

Oh everything can be joined
and tore apart the small prints of his hands and feet.

Like a great mantle about the head and shoulders I got it
set in place because then I could be more comfortable.

This lady holds with one hand the bough of a jeweled tree.

CHAPTER TWO

Around the coal yard, purple iris and white iris were blooming.
He was cutting my hair. "I don't suppose your daughter would
mind if she found you cutting my hair, but somehow it all seems
so clandestine."

He was a big man and self-made. I wondered if he had sewn the
blue and white chintz curtains hanging cheerily at the window
himself. Or perhaps a maid. He seemed to handle things pretty
well although sometimes one could worry about how the town people
felt about things. I have no idea if they ever subjected to scrutiny

the relationship of him and his daughter. However, from appearance she seemed to live a normal life, going out and drinking beer with friends, etc.

Only yesterday I had seen them going from room to room in the Tibetan section of the Oriental museum, studying their very fine collection of scrolls. It had been fascinating for me to note how the large ugly blue power also had its mate clinging to complete it, or sometimes he was fiery red and she was green, her bared teeth near his throat, a string of skulls hanging from his waist.

I was conscious of the fact that perhaps he was trimming my hair too short in back, but he seemed to have his own ideas and perhaps they were better. Not that they were polished in any way, I was astounded at the way he simply seemed to carve with his straight razor around the top of my ear to cut that hair away. I know that it could have been done better but it served the job and soon all was finished.

I somehow felt it best not to presume upon the scene of yesterday for what they looked at in the Tibetan room, I do not know, and my own impressions were confused enough. We talked about his business, the people seemed agreeable enough in the small company he ran, helping themselves to tea when they wanted it and exchanging jokes back and forth. As I said, it was a coal yard, and he had lived there before, simply himself, in a small shack that had been moved several times around the yard and stuck up together again, whereupon he moved in and made a charming but temporary abode. "Simple things for the great folks!" he often used to say.

I began to become uneasy as to his daughter's reaction when she arrived home. "Heavens she won't mind," he said. She always seemed open and cheery but I had heard she suffered dreadfully in a bad romance, and I thought drearily, I hope this all straightens itself out somehow.

CHAPTER THREE

Jack pointed out various strange and ill-made qualities
of the house. "Another layer of wall has been added which you
would have to tear off in order to expose the hot air or heating units
and those are near the ceiling so they would be of no use at all."
"I don't think you need any heat at all, really," I replied. It was a
nice big room, although one must admit a bit ramshackled and
clumsy, since it seemed that without much thought, what had been
two separate units, were joined together to make one house.

We had walked there in the rain to see this show and they
had done a pretty good job of setting it up, although there was that
imbalance I spoke of. Out back it was a different matter entirely,
slats exposed, for a rudimentary floor was all that existed. That
strange cross hatching of slats I had seen used in a similar manner
to build a fire. It was back when I had worked as a nurse for the
two year old daughter of a very famous and well-to-do young couple.

He was a performer who worked
as part of a singing group, and would come home exhausted by the
demands made upon him. One night I could not seem to get myself or the
child to the table soon enough, and exasperated and tired he had just
about decided dinner was not worth the trouble, saying to his wife,
"Come on, let's go to bed," when I arrived with the child and said or
did something, I cannot remember which, that broke the isolation of
weariness from him, and smiling he went out to that funny courtyard of
the house for bottles of wine and vodka. His wife hovering solicitously
near him out back, as he showed us, "Look, three bottles of vodka,"
on the old unfinished planks and rib floor of the courtyard. And over
a fire inside made of criss-cross stakes he cooked a steak, and out the
window and across the valley we could see the lights of the other houses.
I tried my very best to look after and take care of those two, and also
the child of course.

And it is now that I sense the futility of watching and looking after those who really only notice each other. Today it has stopped raining, the vegetable hawkers are outside, the orange flowers have started to fade a bit.

I did not want to take away those ordinary things of mine they did not seem to use well, or used heedlessly, or with indifference, not even knowing they were mine, but placed them carefully back. And they went outside bursting with color off to the beaches and wonderful places. I put them back and I tried to go out too. It is not that I like to give false promises back.

CHAPTER FOUR

When I was living at my mother's house they left me pretty much alone, and I had a whole wing of the house, almost. But after a while I felt that even that wasn't isolated enough and I moved to a large snug room in the basement where I could entertain my friends. I decorated it in blue and was terrifically angry if any of my sisters came down there.

I felt aloof and superior, which I was. On my birthday they tried to give me a party but were making such a mess of it I hurled a large soup plate at them. This disgusted some of my friends, but they were not my friends anyway. When I investigated the refrigerator I found they had eaten most of the cake, I'll be damned if I was going to go canvassing around for it. I took a whole frozen pie.

In trying to make myself more snug, I often had to move entire sections of rooms around, as it occurred to me that this would be better or that would be better, trying to draw it all in, in the best way, around me.

I invited a friend and her young son to stay with me for a while when they were traveling. I tried to keep my laundry separate from theirs. I think the gracefulness of asking them to stay was as far as my sensibilities extended on this matter and I scarcely remember what happened after they arrived.

It is often like that with me. I try so hard to please someone, I often forget where I am or what I am doing. That is why my own real tastes are somewhat of a mystery to me. If one could do exactly as they pleased, in the long run it would make for better harmony and clarity.

CHAPTER FIVE

What I wanted was a meeting between my mother and my friend from the coal yard, but she died. It surprised me. Like a dove lifting from a tree.

I stayed for a while at the house of some friends, but I couldn't play their games, I don't know why my heart wasn't in it. Like dressing up in grand costumes and sitting down to dinner. I couldn't put mine on and hid in the kitchen.

I wanted to put together all the different things I was doing. I took a short trip to get out into some rugged country and walk around. However, as is usual with me, I took a ride when it was offered, and ended up watching some shetland ponies wander behind barbed wire in a run-down park; and listening to furor over whether there was a hole they were getting into and out of.

Jack is my husband. He can see that I fuss over a lot of little panics and he has to see the obvious when the panics become enormous. Nevertheless, any small thing can become a pivot, although likely as not I find I am staring myself in the face. Jack holds up the mirror while I peek and crane about, "I have such lovely ears, I never noticed before, etc." and this can go on for hours.

I saw a real fierce, fat, *mad* pony rush across a rough wide plateau. All four legs in the air at once, and he frowned. It was a lovely place, the sky was all red in the evening. Better take what you need. Bang! Bang! Bang! he thunders along.

CHAPTER SIX

I borrowed a boat from a friend, at least I think that was the arrangement, to take along some of my family and friends. I can tell you, I was relieved when I found out that it was a motor cruiser instead of the sailboat I had half expected for I don't know how I would have managed that. I vaguely thought, one *tacks*, doesn't one? As it was, I got involved with a last-minute guest who was rather famous and I don't even remember who drove the boat at all. The guest, well actually it was Peter O'Toole, was rather drunk, and his eyes were exactly the color of the sea. I do remember, however, that when the boat managed to get stuck on a sandbar, I got down in the water to push it off, all the time worrying if my hair was getting ruined. You should look your best when you hobnob.

That's the way I act, anyway. It's not that I don't watch, anxiously, from the window for Jack to return. But if he combs *his* hair, it's not going to make Mine look any better. I do get people and landscape confused, though. Their route is *their* route.

My friend at the coal yard can be philosophic about all this. If it's water for your teapot you want, take it out of the stream you're next to. The stones, the fish, and the bank aren't necessary.

CHAPTER SEVEN

I was invited to be a bridesmaid at a wedding, or the matron of honor. I didn't know exactly which and the bride didn't either. She was rotund with dark hair and had been adopted. Her adopted mother had been a child prodigy on the piano and she had great gold cabinets full of presents her admirers had given her. She had an egyptian tear vase and had seen Nijinsky dance.

Her daughter was getting married in a real wedding gown, but this was after her mother died. I thought I would wear my white organdy dress I graduated from high school in and later had altered. It was Swiss material my mother had bought in China in the thirties. And a white sweater and white high-heel shoes. After a while I thought this was too summer-like and my chest would look too freckled and white. Besides it was winter anyway so my black dress with the scoop neckline would be better, it was rather bridal looking, at least the neckline was. But then, was black really for weddings? I should have called her and asked her what she thought. But amid all this panic of decision on my part, she changed her mind and decided to have a very informal wedding in the country on a charming little spot next to some caves. As far as I understood then, this meant there were to be no bridesmaids or matrons of honor and I didn't have to worry about what to wear. As this point I had just about stopped speaking to her anyway and besides I had just remembered that she had never shown up at *my* wedding, where I am sure she would have enjoyed herself.

So we all went to the caves, which they had made into a nice little tourist spot, and stood out front, while they got married. "I'm glad *that's* over," said Jack. "I never did like her," I replied.

I met a friend there of the coal yard man's. A rather rabbity librarian who constantly lied about himself, as he was trying to get away with something. I always got immediately involved with him and I had an endless and agreeable chat in one of the lower caves, practically promising my life to him in agreeability until I came to my senses and realized he was as bored as I. I made the first move and left to get involved with the phone calls coming to the bride and groom from well-wishers.

Jack even called a friend of his by mistake. "I think John is trying to get in touch with us," he said. John wasn't, but he was friendly. "My hands are as cold as Philadelphia," he said.

CHAPTER EIGHT

I saw a statue of Athena. She didn't have any head, but you could tell, from the way she stood, what she was like. It was very still.

When you think you know what you expect you still want more. I am surprised when it catches me off base, "But I wasn't *there*." All of the people, all over, mounting and collapsing, and some of them I never hear from again.

It's a different place from where I want to go. I do care if a room is well-made or not, and I don't like the perilous structures, not mine, in the recess of someone else's house.

"There's nothing to fear here, just chatting in the kitchen." I had a conversation with the coal man. "What do you think happened to the cat when the baby sat on it." "Well I suppose she just had her *legs* draped over it and it lay there until she moved."

It was so easy to go racing out and spend my time meandering around some ratty harbor, or getting turned away from the house of an old friend.

"That's right. Just smell the flowers." His daughter came home, and we sat and talked. It was relaxed and friendly and as long as I remembered I wasn't either one of them it was all right.

I was always asking for the specific thing that wasn't mine. I wanted a haven that wasn't my own, and the others knew. You find out when they take you along, all the ill-made parts that make you so scared.

MAY 29

Something sent me back and forth across the room. I didn't find
what I looked for, I didn't know what it was, why did I have
to move.

The clarity of the image. I can't cease talking at the dinner
table. The two things are not related, but I do not know what
to say. In the visual world

I can see them trudging up the hill, I have never been concerned
with the pressure of sounds.

There was a long time in silence. For myself, I can tell you
that certain things give me limited pleasure for short stretches
of time

But I do not know where to put them, they are sure to die, later
than I, being metal or wood, broken hinges and chipped, the horses
step on them, how far can they be thrown and pounded.

"Beauty is so rare a thing." He is weak as I hold his arm he
leans on me as we walk by the ocean. We forgive you for never
giving him the gift he wanted. He died in the park, out
over the ocean he talked of music, it is him I like the best.

I shall not do that again.

July 21. Weedy

you could see the fishes swimming around your legs, also bits
of clear garbage on the bottom. There is a place to go

further, it seems endless. Inside the white-washed room he lies
on the white bed and can see the street. Others come and sit on
a chair by his side to speak, he can't go
any longer with the other old men down to the harbor to smoke and talk.

They watch with large rheumy eyes everyone who goes by, without much
interest, sly old decayed dogs.

                        Like we are sleeping a long sleep
and wake up finally. When they beat the butterflies on the bushes
and make them rise.

THE TREE IN THE FIRE

       It was a young girl

turning, demanding ashes and light. Am I too
    old anymore, too many pinpricks washing away
what were considered false starts, run to check
the houseplants, the cat leaping to the top shelf.
        The tree kept turning
in the fire, its branches burning, the
     tree was burning, 2 months dead, is there a tree spirit
       let loose
inhabits the room for a while.

After the fire was over, it was black. The stove creaked, slightly.
Don't take what you don't want. I looked around at the shimmering.
It did not change or add,
the stiffness in my shoulders, the possibility of any hope, more
logs, more fire burning.

     Now I dress myself to look mellow and dignified,
        tree smoke, nothing changed
        it glows, I am told, more hopefully
   of property
   isn't there anything left?
        To show how the roots didn't get any water
the air didn't treat it right.

DESCARTES AND THE SPLENDOR OF
A Real Drama of Everyday Life.

In Six Parts.

PART I

We are now on an adventure of RIGHTLY APPLYING our VIGOROUS
MINDS TO THE STRAIGHT ROAD, APPLYING OUR REASON
AND SENSE. I shall thus DELINEATE MY LIFE AS IN A PICTURE
so that I may DESCRIBE THE WAY IN WHICH I HAVE
ENDEAVORED TO CONDUCT MY OWN DESIGN AND THOUGHTS
in six parts.

I am not up to subject myself to censure. You may note the grand design
of Yosemite is without flaw, being a natural occurrence. Thus, my
own natural inherited mind has been such. Looming above me in
magnificence, at times leaving me far behind, in short, grandiose above
believability, and in short again, an irritant.

Not being a devotee of the single mind, however, the rapt contemplation
of a pebble in revealing the universal cosmos, I took my lagging
acceptance of my natural magnificence of heritage as being due to the
ignorance and unfamiliarity of my NATIVE COUNTRY.

When it's winter in the corn country people don't stop eating corn.

So I traveled a great deal. I met George, Ebbe, Joy, Philip, Jack, Robert,
Dora, Harold, Jerome, Ed, Mike, Tom, Bill, Harvey, Sheila, Irene, John,
Michael, Mertis, Gai-fu, Jay, Jim, Annie, Kirby, Allen, Peter, Charles,
Drummond, Cassandra, Pamela, Marilyn, Lewis, Ted, Clayton, Cid,
Barbara, Ron, Richard, Tony, Paul, Anne, Russell, Larry, Link, Anthea,
Martin, Jane, Don, Fatso, Clark, Anja, Les, Sue, and Brian.

This being some trip, and the possibilities seeming endless and the faculties
for entertaining and being thus entertained limited, I quit this and
RESOLVED TO MAKE MY OWN SELF AN OBJECT OF STUDY.

PART II

I decided to sweep away everything in my mind and start over again; not adding one little iota until I was absolutely sure of it. I CONTEMPLATE THE REFORMATION OF MY OWN OPINIONS AND WILL BASE THEM ON A FOUNDATION WHOLLY MY OWN. It is impossible to trust any one else. WALKING ALONE IN THE DARK I RESOLVE TO PROCEED SLOWLY.

First of all I am not going to accept anything as true unless I am sure of it.

Second, I divide all difficulties into AS MANY PARTS AS POSSIBLE.

And *Third*, I will go from the easiest to the hardest, in that order.

And *Last*, make sure that I forget nothing.

I THEREBY EXERCISE MY REASON WITH THE GREATEST ABSOLUTE PERFECTION (ATTAINABLE BY ME).

PART III

So my reason may have a place to reside, I thus build myself temporarily a small house of commonly felt rules, a PROVISORY CODE OF MORALS, until I arrive at the grand castle of my PURELY EXECUTED REASON.

I will 1) OBEY THE LAWS AND CUSTOMS OF THE COUNTRY, choosing the Middle Way for convenience, for EXCESS IS USUALLY VICIOUS, and NOTHING ON EARTH IS WHOLLY SUPERIOR TO CHANGE, thus EXTREMES ARE PRONE TO TOPPLE MORE.

2) BE AS FIRM AND RESOLUTE IN ACTION AS ABLE. Once a choice is made, hold to it, thus alleviating PANGS OF REMORSE AND REPENTING.

3) ALWAYS CONQUER MYSELF rather than FORTUNE, and CHANGE MY OWN DESIRES RATHER THAN THE ORDER OF THE WORLD, for EXCEPTING OUR OWN THOUGHTS, nothing IS ABSOLUTELY IN OUR POWER.

> We shall not desire bodies as
> incorruptible as diamonds, but make a
> virtue of necessity in our span of time.

ALL THAT IS NECESSARY TO RIGHT ACTION IS RIGHT
JUDGMENT.
And having furnished my cottage I begin the establishment of the castle.

PART IV

I reject as absolutely false all opinion in which I have the least doubt.
As our senses often deceive us I assume they show us illusion, and must
reject them. As reason is subject to error, and who can offer more living
proof of that than I, I must reject the faculty of reason.
Finally I am aware that I am only *completely* and *confidently* aware of
all this rejection and doubt. This is all I can be sure of, this spinning out
of my head. HENCE I arrive at my First Fundamental Truth. I THINK
hence I AM. OR I Doubt hence I Am; or I Reject hence I am. You get
the picture.
However this *I* is of the Mind, and wholly distinct from the Body. But
then further clear reasoning brings me to this: IN ORDER TO THINK,
IT IS NECESSARY TO EXIST. I never saw a dead man think, I never
hope to see one, but I can tell you any how, I'd rather see than Be one.
Dead men don't think. And therefore, everything we exactly and truly
know, like THE REASONING ABOVE is because it is CLEAR AND
DISTINCT.

I realize that to doubt is a drag, and a PerFECT BEING would accept
everything. But from WHENCE DID I GET MY IDEA OF
PERFECTION!!!!! PLACED IN ME BY A NATURE, BY A NATURE
IN REALITY MORE PERFECT THAN MINE and WHICH EVEN
POSSESSES WITHIN ITSELF ALL THE PERFECTION OF WHICH
I COULD FORM ANY IDEA, that is to say, IN A SINGLE WORD,
MOTHER GOD.
Without this idea of the perfection of MOTHER GOD we should not exist.

Imagination is a mode of thinking limited to material objects. AND THE
STUFFY MIND ASSUMES IF YOU CANNOT IMAGINE, something,
IT DOES NOT EXIST. WHICH IS beside the point and off the argument

if not completely irrelevant to this text by which I am following myself
in glory and splendor. AM I A BUTTERFLY DREAMING I AM ME
or ME DREAMING I AM A BUTTERFLY or am I MOTHER GOD
in Glory and Splendor? Our ideas become confused because we are not
WHOLLY PERFECT and our razor sharp reason must be wielded at all
times to guard against ERROR, error of IMAGINATION and error of
the SENSES.

PART V

THE ACTION BY WHICH SHE SUSTAINS CREATION IS THE SAME
AS THAT BY WHICH SHE ORIGINALLY CREATED.

As I move thru language and transfer the delicacy of vision into the
moving and written word, so all thought not transferred on that level is
lost and degenerated. The animal, the brute, dies a clumsy death for
he is not equal to gods working in man. If they do not speak the language
of man, they speak no language, and are DESTITUTE OF REASON.
That the SOUL WHICH WE POSSESS AND WHICH CONSTITUTES
OUR DIFFERENCE, OUR SOUL WHICH IS LANGUAGE OF
MOTHER GOD WILL NOT DIE WITH OUR BODIES LIKE THE
BRUTES, THE ANIMALS, WHICH HAVE NOTHING BUT THEIR
BODIES TO LEAVE, WE FIND THE SOUL, OUR LANGUAGE, OUR
REASON, OUR MOTHER GOD, IMMORTAL.

PART VI

The difficulties of trusting and using your own mind.
The *I* that is the Pivot, must not wobble, in the name of the established
compendium of minds.
MOTHER GOD has created all, and I found this from MY OWN MIND,
whence reside the germs of all truth.
And from her, THE FIRST CAUSE, comes the sun and the moon and the
stars, Earth, water, air, fire, minerals, porridge.

And from here,
I may explain all the objects brought to my senses. And ALL THE
RESULTS WHICH I HAVE DEEMED IMPORTANT I HAVE
BROUGHT TO YOU, NOT FOR MY PRIVATE USE but for ANY VALUE
THEY MAY HAVE TO THOSE AFTER ME; for our CARES OUGHT
TO EXTEND BEYOND THE PRESENT.
But it is the proof of my own mind's abilities,
any ONE MIND'S ABILITIES THAT MY UNDERTAKING DRAWS
TO PROOF. ONE CANNOT SO WELL LEARN A THING WHEN
IT HAS BEEN LEARNED FROM ANOTHER, AS WHEN ONE HAS
DISCOVERED IT HIMSELF.

Mother God in the Castle, of Heaven.

From this moment
and hence backwards
a visitation
echoes thru the apparent opening
to the tomb
the narrow passage is the mind's reasoning
in clarity
as she moves like a shadow
having lived her life before
it is now the particular graces
that surface
running amidst
that is not lighter than spring
water
is revealed
as the female
opens out
to receive
her own death, which is her own
eternal youth, her own love of herself.

LORD GANESHA

He is in the mountains and in the streams, the fields.
Call upon the Lord Ganesha and he
will appear
immediately
as saviour of grace and belief in the seen.
Observedly
his grace is of love and charm, as I have seen him
with his dainty eyelashes curled
as healer holding
salve, candy!

Now someone led me there, and someone still waits.
That is
I have promised myself attention to them

preserving us. Hymn to the newly found
Breath!
The Spinal Cord up which wanders
the track of energy
in which the whole earth is spotted and moves.

Time was moving out from under us
Nodding and standing still ola
in de Sun
Birthless, Deathless
Oh Man, what a High I was having
Still
illuminating the world of name & form
The Syllable GA represents mind and speech
What is beyond is the syllable NA and by
adoring him in the combination GANA you become
Brahman. This teaching is known as the secret
of VEDANTA

Ponder over it and treasure it and all success
        will come to you,
        becoming the friend of all.

                                Soooo Serious
                        Soooo Gentle
                Soooo full of wisdom
One nods out, gently faints upon the revelation
        of the first thought or so
                into this
on the printed bedspread I look out to sea
        the wind whipping the waves.

        And he is all in the mountains too
                illuminating their intellect.
        For you who suffer, he is Lord of Bliss of Self
        For obstacles hinder us & need only be
                turned aside
        For they are illusion.
                Turn to him, Rodent Mounted
                and you will surmount
                your confusion for he grants
                Quietude to be seen
        throughout by the eye of the intelligent self.

TUESDAY, OCTOBER 28, 1969.
BOLINAS

It was a beautiful golden day
Now a black split shape
          scuttles under
     de foot. So long, Sayonara.
     The fat cat lies down
       dozing. I could use a little rest too
I only slept 11 hours last night,
          wrote some letters, swept the floor,
     planted 2 rows of onions, snow peas
And now I am looking forward
          to washing my hair.

October 28, Take It Easier

I wonder what the ocean is like today?
Cold and flat, hot and flat?
Cold and whippy, tide out, in? The sand
   will be warm, I'm sure
for the sun is out today, and although not warm
in the house
It is in the spot I am going to now.

October 29, Wednesday

In a crowd of people I am suddenly elevated. No matter that
the crowd follows Ginsberg and Snyder, out on a quick
demonstration march thru the halls of a tall building out
into the gardens, their faces among the trees as little
Chinese sages grained into the wood. White walls, somewhat
Grecian, if the fancy takes you. I AM ELEVATING! from a
cross legged position, I rise slowly off the ground in a
crowd of people, easy as can be. ELEVATED! Mr. Ginsberg
and Mr. Snyder frown, not so much? As they are on their busy
way, as groups of people pour their respect and devotion to-
wards them. Pour, pour—they're busy drinking it up all day
in teacups. Do you think we've sent these young ladies and
gentlemen in the right direction? That is to say, haven't
we sent them in the right direction though.
            With my back against a stone wall
in a courtyard, I am closing my eyes and—Now if you will
just observe me, I will move up off the ground, hopefully
as much as a foot, two feet, grind. In my Tibetan bathrobe.
Silence.

Earlier

Into the party, with engraved invitations, I am bored when
I realize the champagne in the decrepit bowl is going to get
filled up a lot. Well then, on the greens in front of the
Mansion are walking Tom Clark and Ted Berrigan, what chums!
Do you think I could possibly fall in step, as they turn same
to far flung university on horizon, gleaming. You bet your
life not. The trouble, says Ted, with you Joanne, is that
you're not intelligent enough.

OCTOBER 31

I am facing an expanse of water. On the other side,
    low mountains rise. And monkey man is leading by the hand
        the earth. Earth spirit face comes out,
      and fly fox spirit, crazy loose dragon
over the range. To maybe scare you? love earth animals?

November 12

Drinking some Coffee—I wonder what
my social calendar is for today.
    And also,
        exactly what I want from Philip in the way of material
for a contrasting design.
            Every exaggeration
           the movement of grass behind the tree
I thought was you
for a moment spacing out.

       Do you know what it was? It was a horse

and that got me away
from wandering city hours fast enough
and a man also
        and here's another one.
I'm totally in a funk
        lounging through Bolinas Streets
and getting ready to do the Laundry.

Noon top social graces.

Thursday, 13 November

Unified School District.
I'm still going to school.
Learning how
to be personal   in the most elevated
State of the Union

MONDAY, NOVEMBER 17

Little bird died
on the seat between us.
not a baby either, up from the south,
gentle dove colored feathers.

I'd take the stronger thing
if I knew how to get to it
and keep on taking it there—see
this is what I'm not sure of,
how it gets lost

But makes you emerge larger
in desire to be there.
Little bird
whose coat now
for a wall.

I get so tired keeping right on
The best intention and pace
brings it all back in
What you are   What you are
What you are

BACK IN TIME

Hurry up and do the laundry
But then of course I have the money

Never talk ahead
      of time
     about
   what isn't.
        This is living
           to give you a present

I walked home & had some soup. Uphill was the best. Play

to as many people as you can.

This is a Short Story
that happened in a short time.
I avoided spending time and reason
on my heart circle. It
ripped me off the wall
and my balance got off
through something not done.
What happened? I pursued, but there
was no direction. How could
I let go of something I didn't know.

No Memory, Right?
Hear how people say what they say piece meal.
Who will show up
Who will go away. My problem heart
was a false me/you. And pursuit and withdrawal
was too much right here. The way
you are pulling it together, a dream.

Communication, I said, is not the word, you are after. That
assumes separation to begin with.
Hear how people have a focus, a guide, go back inside—
Is outside! Dead heart, alive.

JOANNE

The reasonable restraints. This has been

going on for some time. It

takes some time to catch up. First

of all, I look up and am thoughtful

But I'll never catch up. Adding

up all this now I shall proceed. The

pacific ocean is bounding in my eyes,

This sense lays on the surface

rushes of arrivals —descriptions of different

process ease of mind. A little voice

reported on from a minute ago— but

I have just recollected the point

of beginning, which of course

is part of this whole natural

process

drop it away
    they drop away
        when the weight becomes slight
        when the weight is too weighty

That's what
        the devil's all About: Separate

---

beauty then is the final cause
    why we want it
        that is we want it

I wasn't built in a day

    I hope this working out as a novel
approach, at least the disruptions make
the substance. Other wise, inside.

doesn't make any difference
if I've forgotten any thing

The spring
    beneath the tent
        of the sycamore boughs

there, both of them I guess
since our patriarchs' time
    has a nice bench beside it

If you are innocent of heart
    you will sit there and dig it

A little brownie's servant of sand
dances on the bottom
    just a teeny bit up
        from the bottom
    is the top of his moving head

    a rock and a tree
    and some birds

when I couldn't sleep last night

wood
sweep
ocean
music

It's getting figured out

shells
wood
notes

Sunday
will either of them ever awaken
outsleeping each other
Oh Paul my friend, arise!
the vast topples

Monday
war that is Battle
continues
no defeat no Iching

She was a busy body
She kept track
of everything
and did everything
well

You've broken so
many things I have

Penelope

Perfect thought
the relationship of everything
to everything

If you don't want it
for yourself
Don't give it to anybody else

The revolution

when you say <u>know</u>
       I expect you to <u>know</u>

    she convinced herself

       —⊶⊷ ⊶⊷⊷⊶ ⊶⊷—

her head really
            banged
    on the subject

       —⊶⊷ ⊶⊷⊷⊶ ⊶⊷—

Well, eating & pleasure
inside the frame work given us.
    It depends on <u>how</u>
         you killed her

work. it's work

    pleasurable anarchy

Breakfast. He assured me
orange juice, toast & coffee.
Just the way I like it. I flang
the cawfee cup to de floor. After
three times it split into a million
pieces. She worried about the
small supply of dope in the other room.
                        Both
of them, Lewis and Tom, were busy
collaborating. The record
playing. The wind howling
The electric heater going by
her side, as an ache over
increased herself. It was a fact
about what she thought
a moment before, which
was me, it was the love, He's
fine. I wonder why he
doesn't exchange some of
the mescaline for dope. Give Tom
some of the dope.
          I wouldn't go there, into their
minds. I'm here, ain't I. Now
thru the mirror she can see
pine branches nodding nodding
in the blue California sun.

Don't put Your most
    intimate
    in action

Some thing open
Some thing closed

---

2 guys really high up

    high Joanne Hi Joanne

---

but she's wonderful

    and I love her

＊＊＊

          my

      shining star

    and hope

      A place

   where you act it all out

   I mean your thoughts
          should be pure

             oh moon

                   can't get

＊＊＊

   over and over
      until you go
      ahead again

95

when I invoke the moon
it's the best I can find

and all of Bolinas
at my feet

as in your mortal
steps he ate

Can you see you're it
no where you are

fragile, inactive

What on earth to do
Oh Moon

Oh Moon
from the sea, the blinding blinkers
lights on a dirt road
I am always right

Oh Moon walking home on the dirt road
walking on moon space
what my mouth says

don't do this—don't do that
don't ride a horse
too long

Oh Moon
That's all I know

Well I didn't want you to leave
        green foot steps grown
      older a bit by old knowledge
            as light
      no time   is the right time
bands of iris
clumps of nasturtium

                    In California
I am in Paul McCartney's new house
      2 floors, paneled in wood
          It's oak he says
        what kind of oak do they
      have here,
                  Sherman Oak.

doll's house
sighing high over the
branches voices
of the children music

Well I just want you to
know the truth

he makes love to her
　　he talks about
　afterwards
　　when some years
　ago
he worked
　　for the welfare
　department
　　　in New York City

She starts up
　a hue
　　and cry
　oh the money, the electricity
　　give me
　　　some clothes, some jewels
　　　　some food, some love

in the corner
don't you worry

The tunes, familiar
weeping & laughing
I leave my love behind

what I wanted to say
was in the broad
sweeping
form of being there

I am walking up the path
I come home and wash my hair
I am bereft
I dissolve quickly

I am everybody

You write from the inside
        traveling
                in a 3 quarter length skirt
        go to sleep
        go to sleep

a life time

what happened
it stopped

It's always free
It's always easy

1970 SUMMER BOLINAS

Still
          our breath our sun
     our moon, our stars, our space
     our water that flows
out of the mountain, our ocean, our roads, our paths
               and into this year and into the next
               into the warm grey day, the damp smells rising
     up out of the earth.
                    See, we can learn to move gracefully
               through this past learning.
          This is a dream about 2 sources
               of image and language
                    about strength and ease
     green tips that are fingers
     pointing to the sky.
               In the sun in the mist
          on the hill across
                         I remember spring now in summer
               in sun petals
                    the quick grass springs back, a vehicle
          for what passes through
Not for identity of I's and sorrows
          Struck by humility total of truth
     Listening to separate existence of worlds
          since I was born
               To look at the substance
          of what passes by the eyes
                         sparkling
          in pages of notes of music
          and remain in memory as renewal,
     as voices from out on the water

as craft
that carries this voyager forward, Back
out of time, is this moment
when I write to you
these notes of myself

Not Yet

Not tomorrow night
but the night after
   tomorrow
Not tomorrow
   but the night after
   tomorrow
Then the moon will be full
Then the moon will be full

It's been a long time

NOTES FROM THE REVOLUTION

During the beat of this story you may find other beats. I mean
a beat, I mean Cantus, I mean Firm us, I mean paper, I mean in
the Kingdom which is coming, which is here in discovery.

It is also Om Shri Maitreya, you don't go across my vibes,
but with them, losing the pronoun. It is Thy, it is Thee,
it is I, it is me.

Machines are *metal*, they serve us, we take care of them. This
is to me, and this is to you. You say you to me, and I say you
to you. Some machines are very delicate, they are precise, they
are not big metal stampers, She made enough poetry to keep
her company.

My Vibes. You intercepted my vibes. The long shadows,
the long shadows, the long shadows. My sweet little tone,
my sweet little tone is my arm.

On what Only: The song that girl sang the song that girl sang

NEWS BULLETIN FROM KEITH LAMPE

Soon

Little Neural Annie was fined $65 in the Oakland
Traffic Court this season for "driving while in
a state of samadhi". California secular law requires
that all drivers of motor vehicles remain firmly seated
within their bodies while the vehicle is in motion.
This applies to both greater vehicles and lesser
vehicles.

DESECHEO NOTEBOOK

Desecheo

off   West Coast   Puerto Rico
1½ miles long
1 mile wide
the end point of
an upheaval that happened
in the Caribbean

•

forest steep ridges   gumbo forest
limbo

what's between a hill
& a mountain

•

no water   tree holes
goats   cactus
monkeys
boobies   domestic cat
crabs   tidal pools

a species of great beauty

they have auras

Travel Broadens

a little Revery

      Shao, John Thorpe, and I are in this room and
I am sewing. Where ever he is, in the room, his presence
is known to me.
        The piece of paper napkin
        actually a yellow paper towel
        upon which Peter
        has the number and name
        of the boat man
            our only transportation to the island
        is thrown in the waste basket
        by my desk
        and then out of the trash
        down stairs
        and into my purse
        where it still is.   In San Juan
        the only location
        of information
        besides the front cover
        of the Creeley's phone book
        in Bolinas
                Friday

Tuesday

What living on an Island is all about.
                    housing
        for hermit crabs.
                the eel, Ray,
                        cats
the dish water food.
bamboo spoons

            I am a foul temper. Inside
I have this conversant world, those I am intimate
with I allow to share
                Elizabeth arrives.

What   goes   on   in   the   mind   imagination.   Writing.
                        Speech and conversation.
                        That story.

            Prisoner of Zenda.
    Milarepa. Houdini. The magician's fire.

Wednesday. I am alone. Everything is tidy.
at the swimming pool a cool
breeze.

Writing. I am a writer and a talker. I get hungry too.
    I just plucked my eyebrows. In order to alleviate
    a sternness. Especially around my eyes, which
    show my age. I have reminded myself not to

frown or grimace as these are unpleasant faces
and ugly.

I wish to have a smooth countenance.
I want to be behind this face and proud of it

drifting thoughts.

Dave (and Elizabeth) caught 2 fish.

Monday

styrne

sternness: an essay on

Well as far as I know. Down the beach Bill
Sargent, Stewart; and one other is he Mickey Sam or
Jerry hammer Sternly. That's silly. They're in the
shade. With my determination I wanted to talk in the
abstract. OK now I'm down to business. Dictating this
tone. This tone is right now. Good lord I think I may
have buried some Tampax over there. There is the
son of the governor of Massachusetts turning over a
rock and looking sternly down. Gracious. We won't
mention that I'll just have to accept it as my kismet
on this desert Island stumbling around on rocks look-
ing for the ultimate lady-like way for the perfection
of toilet.

There is a main street in this town. Wait Wait I don't want to eat myself. In this small white house with 2 bedrooms over on the Poplar side of Callagy's land lives my mother. Is there room for Philip Whalen there?

On this Island at one time were thousands of goats. See, I am not afraid. I cling to the small pool. The rest go out in the boat. Only human beings, after all, though they are all men.

See. I am walking in a dream again and want to see sharp focus. The monkeys have their drama in the hills. And Tom who watches has the belief in their story. A new Baby.

There is an old sword in those hills I mean the hills are not that many but it cried when the fisherman tried to pull it from the ground. Where upon he ran away. And the sword was never seen again.

Dying in the maritime zone; this part that goes down to meet the sea's edge; where N-V Envy a young prince who lost a battle for power died. Sadly in a cave.

A red Cape.

green shoes.

I will lay briefly only on this question of why. It is the beginning of rot. Hacking briefly with the diamond sword. The dawn comes up like Thunder out of Mandalay. This is a thought. Thin bands of clouds across the moon.

So cool in the early morning, here.

Tuesday March 16

Maybe if I change the point

of departure.   Lorraine Barrow,   Nancy Borgstrom, Suzanne.

This youth who stays away all night. Shows up, a juvenile delinquent. Where they are shooting bullets across the narrow passage into the store house.
A path by the ocean.
Ocean shore, train station, great house. Road to town

Hunch back whales, big white breakers
out to sea
Three

Peter has a tooth ache and may leave
the island.

Psychotherapy is not the
application of method.

The 'psyche' is not
a personal but a world existence.

The kernel of all jealousy
is lack of love.

water into wine. is.

Concepts promise protection
from experience.
The spirit does
not dwell in concepts   Oh Jung.

Peter said yesterday, looking at his
glasses in the pocket of his shirt, I'm so
glad I haven't lost my glasses. And
then he lost them.

Pearly
Pearly
Pearly

the Sound the voice

Wednesday night
The Sun is going down
The Clouds are an igloo in front
Big rays shoot above

Evening Madame   says   Sam as he walks
down the main path past my house. I am
sitting on the front porch.
It will be nice when it
gets red, says Stewart, who is from
Mill Valley and measured breasts in
New Guinea. Oh goody says I.

I said, OK, I want to have a talk with my unconscious
as I walk up and down the concrete helicopter pad.
This figure will come up that I will commune with.
Maybe the king of the monkeys. He will come right
down out of the hills with all his noble group. Floating
breast bone shapes. Exaggerated and dancing figures.
I promenade the landing field. Enjoying my walk
springing up and down in a street walk. I'll tell every-
one at dinner. Meanwhile under the god bless America
sky is coming a twister and out there, look, a whale.
Two people offer Peter his glasses. Just hold these
down, just keep track, says Tom rushing off in the
Whittamore strut elbows high.

Thursday

I am in bed with Jack. Peter
comes in. Oh you 2 take care of it.
            Superman's low flight.

It's me too observing the dwellings by
the train station as I fly by, carrying
someone to this hotel room in Spain.
Lee and Anne Adair.

            When spring comes to the
ocean eggs.

            History of the Island, this
movie, subjective feelings and objective
actions.

            He exists outside time & is the son
of the maternal unconscious.

Friday

Visiting Gary's house last night. The sleeping bags are close at the top of the road; so the hermit crabs won't get in. He lives on an island in front of a black lake. This Island is 80 miles long he says. I know the shore. His son, Kai, out among the boulders in the black lake. In the house, a very nice one, the dishes are not done. Masa is sitting on the floor. Here she says later, handing out a pot of poi, are some eggs and bacon. Gary is also cooking a pot of goo too. The house has two floors, although somewhat dark, and later it is perched high in the mountains where it belongs.

Dave's dream: for a wedding present a big picture of Peter with a black band under it, given by his brother and his wife and a friend named Doug, a financial combination. Please peel off the black band. It says *congratulations*. Under that it says *a house in the country*. The picture of Peter peeled gets bigger and bigger.

Saturday

Tom says You got me
Stewart says Silence speaks

So many things happened. Being with this life
form that is Peter. This belief in life from my tangled
roots, which left me only my own faith to decide. And
this spirit keeps the delicate thread spun so finely over
and over thru the centuries, past back over the Greeks.

Delicate for it is so long and finally spun.

And this man speaks
to me, of the creation of life. The Sun, the night, this
earth with its finely gathered garment. For I thought
for a while we were the new race being born.

I was no longer in waiting as this world I called
my own opened out.

Monday
The lord is gracious
Beloved
Rock
Elisheba

I thought
You said

way laying

I want to go back
I want to get back
        out of this
fairy tale land.
            Sure I lie to you from
                what I want to hide
            and I am clothed

                so the high high voice
                is like an Air

        The Crab kingdom
            my Cracking Dome

            The big blue carpet
            unfolds

My total belief
            was so great
    at the occasion of that moment
        all directed towards
    the belief in the capacity of what I see

            This write often

he played the harp
      and I lay in the bathtub
            chanting
OM
forcing my way
only love's hurried urgency

Thursday

      the quality of mind
like I am keeping track of
3 or 4 people at one time
    bathing naked
A letter to Bobbie Creeley
  no place to sit
all these men
    I just want a place
for myself

Saturday

> OH fish of the sea
> die happily

> OH the sea comes in like the mighty
> bread and fish

Besides Tom and Peter, Sam Burr
is left on this island. The others
left Thursday when Tom came back
from St. Kitts. Someone stole the
head of N - X. The hermit crabs having
cleaned her bones. An open address
by Peter. Who has stolen her head,
I'm going to search their luggage.
To be left in her natural place.

She rose up in the white raiment
    the feminine spirit escaped
        as the body began to lose
            its life.

Sometime ago caught
        rammed through with a spear
and still lays dying
        in a black plastic bucket
        flopping over
            the sign
        I sing
        OM Sri Maitreya
            what for the soul
        of a dying fish
    stick a knife in its brain
now it is meat, fish meat

Sunday

I know I do not suffer more than anyone
        in the whole world
But this morning I had to have first thing
        2 cigarettes, half a joint,
        a poached egg and corned beef hash, 1 piece toast,
                                        2 cups tea
        Jung, Williams, shells, stones,
                2 slugs rum, depression, rest of joint,
        cigarette, 7 Up, and it's only 10 o'clock
Because I wanted to write a poem
Because I want something to come out of me
You can't try. I believe in life, I am living
        now and for a moment the landscape
                becomes clear.

A home, a house. I talked with Jack Kerouac
        last night. We were sitting under
                a rack of clothes, as if it were a clothes
        closet. There goes Keith Lampe in a white coat
        with blue braid. He's something, isn't he.
                We agree, we are discussing.

Now there are three large wire enclosures, one with
        a wire roof, like they had been tennis courts.
A group of uninformed nature people,
        have decided to dump the whole zoo
        into these courts, getting the
        birds into the one with a top. But OH!
they are inept. The animals can't live together
peacefully. All the jaguars, leopards & ocelots
        take out after a rabbit. How did I ever
        condone the action of these people. Such naïveté

The more I slow down the harder it is
to all of a sudden move again.
    Smaller & smaller until the
    speck in side dwindles so small

Generosity: I allow
　　　　your existence
　　equal weight with mine

I kick the rock
　　　　Rock spirit come out
　　　　damn it

　　slowly a string
　of beautiful figures drift
from the cave
　　　　high up on the rocks
　　riding through the mists
their diaphanous clothes
　　　　flutter
　　in the grey breeze

There was a time
　　　　when I wanted
　　　　to learn the knowledge
out there
possessed by the world

　　　　it helps on this island
　　to do exercise
　　　　thoughts stay
　in the mind close
to the home camp

Monday

Main street has been wiped out
the sea is pouring in

OH. They're like rushing horses
    OH. Look at this
       Balloons
         Bows of silver
        Bowels
                you are sitting like the stone monkey
Lilies of the Valley
      Blue
What is beautiful Joanne what is beautiful

      Discipline
    we are short on supplies
  I've already smoked
             one of tomorrow's
     3 cigarettes
           OH
      This is incredible
        Big pounding waves
    the beginning of my 4th week
        here
       the gold light of
         late afternoon
      A big heron
        stops
     fine milk foam
       rise up and pound
   This was a flat sea

Tuesday

         boulders
     breakers in the clear
blue sky

Peter's rucksack got swept away last night
   at dusk
      by 30 feet dark silver monsters
    It was life or death when they started to rise.
I grabbed Sam's muffins from the table
     and put them in the block house.
Calm down said Peter as I started to laugh
     madly. Put sensible things away
     like these boots under the table. OK.
Peter bounds down the beach. With great
     sounds. Like the last lap of a relay
     as the last of Sam's structure began
     to tumble.
A grating roar the foam sucks back
   and Peter's rucksack and all his papers
      rush out too.
      Margot Doss's hiking boot.
Waist deep in foam
His papers I collect busily & tidily,
the second sea bath for his Thesis,
     monkey papers, Golem, notebook
       in 2 pieces
    while the next tidal wave
      prepares to come in

Sam battles neck deep in foam
        but loses possession
            of Peter's rucksack
        which also has Keith's camera in it
            and the last of my cigarettes
        besides everything else he
                owns.
                gone.
Now you will hate me says Peter.

I strongly sense I will not leave this Island alive.

                                        Phoebe MacAdams had
                                         her baby last night.

Wednesday

    Pat Haines. A new neat town, colony. In parts of the
town the houses are all black. Like it was strictly formal
or maybe Harvard. Climbing down from the top roof
the steps, which Peter goes down first, are without a
doubt steep, almost vertical, & narrow, both in width
and breadth.
    It is impossible. I am sad. I am scared. No rails. But
there are bars over the window one passes, to hold on
to. And I get down in a rush. Shiny black shoes.

              The head of N - X
                was found by Tom
                  in the deep underbrush

              All that stood accused
                  of head theft
                are now innocent.

              The accuser stands
                  revealed.

Thursday April 1

  grey day
   at 10
waiting for the coast guard cutter
   packed up
    onions left over

an arrow in the form
of an arrow

   Landed by helicopter

I am still alive
smelling of the ocean

   news of Bolinas

     Friday's nature

      can a *wild* animal
      exist anymore

       wilderness

     words. spirit guides

     further away
      into crammed people land

      New York

       MARCH–APRIL 1971

The rain
is soft, gentle
big whales rush up from ocean bottoms
and travel in families
Shooting their big bodies out
into the air

FALL 1971
Bolinas

Bird family
boat going out to sea
all this
every day

This is the way I like to feel the best.

Out the window
the birds are feeding
and they are jumping in the puddle
the hose makes
on that hard ground
outside the front
of the house
some flutes
from Peru.

This is the way I like even better doing nothing at all.

I want to point out that I am not up tight

I am not up tight

Often I try so hard with stimulants
   which only graze the surface
  like I wish to become surface

Whereas the real state is called golden
   where things are exactly what they are

   Utmost Disarray

 Get Out of Here

     Out of

 MY WAY

No one was watching the tortillas.

You were.

That's my new name. No One.

That's my new name. No One.

Now this tiny pause from my bursting brain

I am Beautiful. This is my name

             See I am It. I am getting It.
    I am the big rolling, breathing, sliding
sighing, lifting   -
             Ground!

I want a smaller thing in mind

Like a good dinner

I'm tired of these big things happening

They happen to me all the time

Oft have I wondered and climbed

the blue green forest ranges.

Oh this is not true

Oh you know

myself at home

these dusty greens in yellow

TRIP OUT AND FALL BACK

We left to the East in a drive away car. Driving
all day, and a lot of the night, we stop only
at Blue Mesa, in Arizona, striped in blues and greys.

The galley is the back of the car—cucumbers, grass,
and cheese, get passed up and around. Going right
through on the big highways is space travel, watching
only the number signs. In the South we are fearful,
but survive with heavy fried oysters. Millions of
governors' palaces. My grandfather in a graveyard
in Virginia. Through the Blue Ridge Mountains,
Peter throws the Upanishads out the window and we have
to go back and get it. Until we arrive in Brooklyn.
Enjoy, says Peter's mother, and we do, in this boyhood
home, on the tree lined street.

In this endless dream of parties, Gordon Baldwin
drives a tractor across the field. I am watching
John Thorpe and his drinking buddy, Angelica Clark,
standing by the pool table at the side of the field.
How can you be monastic and drunk at the same time,
she says, and advocates a return to Protestantism
as the Middle Way.

At the corner store they could buy flowers. I was not
sure if I liked her but I chose to be delighted. Always
worried about my colors, some implicit shabbiness.
Whereas she was younger; and ambition and belief,
charming and loving; whereas poetry bereft was my best
friend. There was the happiness of friends from
long ago when poetry was my husband and my bride.
So peyote made me very careful of the religious
moment, and I knew these times to be timeless. His
old mother was dying, but they all knew that, I guess.
And I wanted romance; the clear and graceful design
that embroiders all, the natural harmony of the eye.
I return again to the mussel shell on the roof top
restaurant, under the warm summer stars; and above
all the return to Brooklyn where I lay in his room
full of stories and books.

We went over to this party at a loft
after Rick called up to see if it was
all right. All right! We didn't even
stop to eat. Peter carried Joan piggy-
back as we ran along and they both
collapsed at the curb along side tall,
dark buildings, but picked themselves up
for the hell bent drive to get to another
place. It was a going away party for a
pleasant dark faced man. Everyone sat
in a circle on the floor and smoked the
perennial dope. I drank as much wine
as I could. Sydney went to the refrigerator.

The host was success bound, even though I
was nice to him, and thought our Puerto
Rican music should be put in the furnace.
It sounds like it's from 14th street,
he said. That's right. I told everyone
I was giving a poetry recital. They smiled
politely.

I sat on a children's chair and watched
Jasper Johns turn into a Chinese man. In
a dark pool of port, in a puddle of pot, in
a Tibetan posture, long hair around the corner.
Are you all this self awareness and ego? For
sure, Chenrezig. Whether it was in my purple
mini skirt from Lynn and my blue sandals from
Phoebe, or the yellow beads from Bill, or
Joe's brown silk bandana. Or the book stores;
or the Attaining of Intuitive Wisdom.

He at times had a way of rolling his hips
in a moving way. Rollicking and solemn
the Tibetan pictures are brought out.
Yes I know that guru and I know that guru also.

Oh tell me the story
Oh New York, grandiose and kind of place
I see your tiny green trees peeking up
        Along about twilight
        In the moon whorls

———— ◦◦◦◦◦ ◦◦◦ ————

        The vibes are too high
        They're Empire State high
        I'm a ground hole watcher
        Out my Bolinas window

Whether I belong one place anymore
than another

•

Get out of here

•

All the vibes hit me different

•

Large westerner

Dick said this is a skidoo bridge. As
we were walking in his woods, on an overcast
New Hampshire Sunday. I thought he meant
for the kids to get away fast, off his property,
into the next woods. But he didn't like
this homemade bridge, and his dog Cybele proceeded
to rip it apart. E.S.P. A way to find
your way back. She gnawed, like a cob of corn,
the supporting rails until they fell away
into splinters.

Gordon, for example, is tall, with dark hair, often
worn in varying lengths, mostly with glasses. And
sometimes a mustache. His rooms are of dark redwood,
and his eyes are even with the cypress tree tops.
When he does things, he does them very well. And
he always keeps himself neat, plus he has a marvelous
sense of humor, which is more than I can say about
most people. He is also very formal. And I mean
by formal that he pays close attention to all his
actions, plus he always lights a lady's cigarette,
and even offers one, although she has been bumming
them for years. Once when he walked into a party
half the room sighed Oh Gordon, like a breeze, oh
wonderful. The other half wanted to be introduced
immediately. He has a fine sense of fitness,
gardening a lot, and even wearing neckties.
          It was on Gordon's balcony
that the word 'ambience' first arrived. I have also
seen him, in the presence of his father, meticulously
polish his shoes with a tooth brush; and here
that's a heavy action.

Compassion flows forth like the well of surrender.
Effective, the reins of radiation
from the nestling arms of comfort, cross legged, etc.
In which the obliteration of restraints
In which the obliteration of restraints
cause the room to become spaceless
hurtled far above the buildings.
The sad pavements covering trails by foot on earth,
the lone squirrel walking down Canal Street
looking for a tree,
While Art flourishes so energetically in people made
            people made environments, Man's testimony
that the fruits of man's creation will be received by man
and paid, and hung upon, and listened to, and read,
and looked at

Held to be exhausted and deranged.

Is this order ever ceaseless? Like the grey sky
the seedy bamboo, cypress in bloom with yellow
                              ladened boughs.
We have met the enemy and they are ours.

                    I love you all,

                         Joanne

Peter Rowan and I are walking down Mesa Road.
He asks me who are my teachers. I don't want
to mention Mrs. Hoefer across the street.
I tell him Bill Berkson and Arthur Okamura
are my teachers.

These several selves that move one self around, thousands
jiggling. It is so inappropriate to be unfound, whine
around, hesitate, lock the window again, this body is
dissipated. To accomplish, to learn, with thanks, to one's
past history is brought up close. And for a while, with
late spring's wild radish flower blooming past my window,
the further shore is close, is here. I do not want to say
he is dead yet because he has not yet come back, but my
sadness for the missing comes recognised, is acceptable.
Gone with the last look he questioned me with. Have you
done this to me?
                    Indeed are they my forces or the forces
I am within. That no children come from me to love. And I
am this space in time, this focus, of articulation, that hears
the bee buzz round and round.

I have large dreams of beautiful patterns.

Clouds over Indiana
And we are under them

Who even said I was a poet. Because I write
this down. I want bullet-like speed and precision
to show that this mind connects in ways of delight, and
also says truth way beyond this individual voice.
Thus I speak from the holy story, the ordinary story.
Thus I am married to the household gods, thus I aspire
to be the consort of heaven. Thus I am sad when the earth
is from me. We sleep together again. In no way will I
part from this union. And the sky who is my father
opens the world of the golden kingdom.

                        Even if I repeat what others say,

it becomes mine.

The famous Utah mountains embroidered in gold, russet
& pink.
                LET YOUR SELF GO.

One thinks 'the obvious'. You say it sounds so obvious.
I wanted to do something I called writing.

                I think you've done it
                It's finished *now*.
                It's a new map
                  in a delicate space
                For what once was growing there.

                                  FALL 1972

A small field of tall golden headed grass, heavy with seed
    at the top
Why did I travel so far away from you who wishes to be
    snug in her home
The grotesqueness of this California woman who wishes
    to take off her clothes but instead displays herself in
    provocative attitudes
Wrapping my shawl about my waist I went into sparkling water
    on shale reef.
    I am not empty
Small sea anemones show their pink and blue insides.
Everything I walk on is alive.

There is something in me which is not open,
        it does not wish to live
           it is dying
But then in the sun, looking out to sea,
        center upon center unfold, lotus petals,
the boundless waves of bliss

September

The grasses are light brown
and ocean comes in
long shimmering lines
under the fleet from last night
which dozes now in the early morning

Here and there horses graze
on somebody's acreage

Strangely, it was not my desire

that bade me speak in church to be released
but memory of the way it used to be in
careless and exotic play

when characters were promises
then recognitions. The world of transformation
is real and not real but trusting.

Enough of these lessons? I mean
didactic phrases to take you in and out of
love's mysterious bonds?

Well I myself am not myself.

and which power of survival I speak
for is not made of houses.

It is inner luxury, of golden figures
that breathe like mountains do
and whose skin is made dusky by stars.

O fresh day in February
      Come along
with me under pine whose new cones
          make flowers. In a mellow mood
      let's take anything
    and you're better
in the peaceful flowing
in the beach
in the bird who flies up
     out of coyote bush,
       bob cat who crosses the road.

   For who could think *I* could see
the grace of other souls born, and reborn
      before in crab shells
    snail shells, the head of a grebe
   moleskin, new onions up. Drawn by
your clever sleigh of tortoise
      I listen for the melody
     to sing along

Every day I burn a stick of incense
in front of
Kannon San. She is Kwan Yin
she is Avalokiteshvara. This is what
I know about some of her names.
She holds a bottle
in her right hand
by her side and has the other hand
raised up. This she does
consistently
and without stopping. I have read
about her but can't remember
it as really important

for how she affects me
as a dark little statue
I make an intelligent
pass at, when I bow
I mean I am hopeful
she evens off the demons.

Oh holy Mary
how come you come
into my words
I was born with
and on the radio too.
Oh holy Mary
you'll just say
I'm not a good enough
Christian
to go to heaven &
you look so sad
You are merely human
and wafted above us

the Queen of a big
church who staked out
the real estate
But then again what do I know
of my heart but that it is tight
and wishes to burst
past the wall of my chest

I am depressed, darling
the power of belief
is from me

When I used to focus on the worries, everybody
was ahead of me, I was the bottom
of the totem pole,
a largely spread squat animal.

How about a quick massage now, he said to me.
I don't think it's cool, I replied.
Oh, said he, after a pause, I should have waited
for *you* to ask *me*.

The waves came in closer and closer.

When I fall into the gap of suspicion I am no longer here.

In this world that has got closed over by houses
and networks, I fly out
from under the belly. Life's dizzy crown
of whirling lights, circles this head. Pure
with wonder, hot
with wonder. The streets become golden. All
size increases, the colors glow, we are in myth.

We are in easy understanding.
Scarcely talking, thoughts pass between us.
It is memory. As I search to find
this day's sweet drifting. The fog out to sea, the wind.

This is the first time I have had peace
in days, she told her assembled friends
later on, in the afternoon

The breath played in and out
of his harmonica, as he passed

under the grove of eucalyptus
in Oggly-Boogly Land

But why
does he want to do that, write down
all the road signs from here
to the east coast

or all the names of flowers
in order to put them down
in favor of a magnificent
You, who is his wife. These two poets

like what they do, I am sure
but I hardly get touched
anymore, with all the books
and what, for reading.

Just a little bit
does the magic AHHHH
come out and let itself be heard
all round about

I don't believe in any
of your gods or powers
It's all Bullshit

I don't even believe
in My powers or gods

Her dying words were
Keep the house clean

The far off pine whose branches turn yellow
is saying goodbye, and its needles fall
even this June. The blue meets the cloud
banks coming up late afternoon. Radish
flower, coyote bush, the old
stove rusting—were that it would fly
on little wings to the Pt. Reyes Dump.
Oh I am so tired, in this little room,
trying to open
the path of rhythm with rhythm, positively
breathing

When I was well into being savored, I didn't want
to pick about the bits and pieces of sociality.
Friendly, but moving smoothly into other places, my
pen, my staff of life was gone. Nothing in the way,
I speedily took to new roads.

So where have I gone to and where have I come from.
We smoke a joint and share a can of beer. Primitive
man was the first man, but is not valued on a level
of progression. We're always in touch, you see.

And he leaned across the table and spoke to me. It
was a visitor that placed value on everything I have.

                        But then I let the
smaller more tender fantasies take along much of my breathing
daylight moments alone. The desire to reveal myself takes
me from one group to another, and with sad longings I
place it on the table to serve. I tell my complaints.
I intricately recite the details of the day and the
possibilities of what they mean. Yet I know though this
time passes pleasantly, it has ended all possibilities
of creation, for it has all been done. But then again
this news is affirming for it clusters richly, densely,
and how I want to be heard!

And will this plot of the house never be completed?
Earwig skitters across my desk! Oh Lord, the possible
bells ringing, to bring me out of here.

When I step through the door
everything has changed. Finally,
  it is out the door
  past homes, down the trail
  the lovely beach
    draws me into her drawing. Finally

I am past the fear of life's paucity.
Green Angels, stream, in hot California
and in the stillness seeds popping.

In my imaginary conversation with you 2, tears
well up.
         It is all fantasy, garbing, to make
an agreeable arrangement of senses. I love it. It makes
things easier. Is nature sad? No, it's playful,
and to say the least, dramatic. You are alive! And so is
my refrigerator, that sings a long, with Maria Muldaur.

May the darkness come down upon you! There is no way
to make you happy in the future. But the same
insistent drama shakes itself outside. I am
your friend. I wasn't even taught to be this way,
but gained it. And it is all at this point,
that my success comes out to you.

                              Bits
of dried grasses pinned to a wall. She makes
herself, decorative, agreeable, for him. They nod
inside a flower, a wonderful room.

I thought I would never get out here again
The months
have not been unkind, all the possibilities
of days leaving us open, to something I never got at
but talked about, the service of unity.
                    And no I don't have no
pressure, and certainly I don't do anything. So
much I want to drift, into story land, take life
a little easier.

It is true, there is power within us. But I am so
improperly trained. Mostly it is
get your own 'thing' going, facing
each day's rise and set.

                       Maya, Maya,
on de foot afternoon.

I am veering closely back and forth

Oh! Half moon behind the slim holder of the lotus
Oh! she's a poet. Joanne Kyger
Who was that woman?
Oh come over and visit.
Oh it's all passed, gone, gone, gone.

Looking out to the garden fair
Come comb my hair.

This is mere writing built on paper,
The mysterious help from our friends
    transcends this all. Thus whatever
You do best allows *me* more
    ways takes
me into living's glad hands.
        Ah, but the day shifts so remorselessly.
And things to do, the eternal things
            to do traps
        speculation, traps
our deepest bass drum, the heart.

It's a great day. Last night I visited my old
childhood town of Lake Bluff, Illinois. The
Creeleys and Philip Whalen were there. I took
a walk to Lake Michigan with Philip to see it all
built up in the form of a great amusement center.
Lost in its intricacies I go to work. Stepping out
a door I land in a great field and run a tractor up
and down the rows, not exactly enough, to be sure
and run back into the amusement center, donning my
waitress uniform on the way, before I get caught,
before I get caught. Oh Ladies of the Middle West,
how do your hands get rough. What is this self
I think I will lose if I leave what I know. Back
to the dark bedroom, and aimless unhappy adolescent
lives. Lacking any commitment to the actual living
ground, life becomes pointless in its urge for culture,
quote unquote, Art. There, I've said it, in all its
simpleness—the best teacher lives outside, the best
teacher lives inside you, beating blood, breathing
air, the best teacher is alive.

Wooden walls make us a nice little palace
with ancient roar down the the street
and mulched pine and mountain lilac
Outside the door I'll walk for wild iris
today away

Of all things for you to go away mad on a tender morning like this
although grey for the 8th day in sunny california
because I asked you to change your shirt after the third day
because the neckline won't come clean
and you said you preferred dirty necklines
and I hurled the pancake turner to the floor
shouting what about appearances
and you said it took a long time to see through appearances
   and what do we care
   and you got no breakfast, no pancake, forget it. I hope
      you eat some lunch.
          And at 12:30 you still got no lunch which information
via the phone I find out because I want to tell you I am sorry
about the pancakes and appearances, grey day, the Pride of Madeira
fallen over in the garden. Plucked and plummed, all show, no heart,
heavy headed, no answer, breathe deeply.
                    Enough of slumber land. I've put
                  beans on for dinner
We'll sit at the table, and don't put me on, the room in my heart
gets nourished, by your friendly handsome looks. You read
a lot of books.

The apple tree bludgeoning, this hot day after rain.
Oh every thing is growing, even too high. We're still
here, the apple tree planted two
years ago.
        I wrestled with the dragon
who holds the diamond jewel
                of liberation. It came out
"wander in the big dome of living tissue."

    Chill waves of reason, days move under us

as I go over them

Throwing a crank in the monkey wrench

Now that it's practically over I have arrived. That's fine.
I'm full
of French ideals. Which happen way before the case
the next time around. So I do, what I want to do.
Which in many cases is chicken or not enough. The POWER
of the voice and so on. A little bruised and wounded
at bottom in the poor breath. All heaped and huddled
over in a prayerful position with the head
pressed to the earth.
                    Just resting and dreaming.
About planets and people, the primitive, new woman.
          Who sits with her breath daily.

                    Struck with the chill
reason of death I get the cold
               departure.

               Steam at a low
                 a war starts
                    "I hate you"

Ear ringing supplies to the body. Fuel chuga-chuga.
               14 telephone wires go by
          our house.
                    Big machines do the sewer ponds.
          I sit strong with thoughts
          of paradise
     streams running out
                    to big ocean rush.

Is this the Buddha?
That individual will die
that day dream
Individual.
And you
secret one, watching, watching all the time
or at least some of it
in a set up from the wings
See the truly enlightened other. Thank you.
It's me.

I don't want to repeat
the same mistakes over again,
or the mistakes somebody else made just so
I can have the experience of them. See, fucked
up again. Live and learn. And off the excessive
fondness for one's own self knowledge, un-
tested, but reigning supreme. That leads me
more astray, every day. What we commonly
know in the air, in our dreams, what chooses
continually & continually to grow, the obvious
under our noses, is this life. Yearning is blind-
ness. The weed has a name, is quite proud of it-
self, builds a community with other weeds, birds
hop through. The imported domestic is a labor
of love, but a labor, such a labor. At home here,
no single thought is my thought. It whispers
through the air in sweet misty fog,
in bright sky blue.

April 4, 1975   Time of wonder
on how it goes together. And pausing to see.
            The same landscape only changed
by progression of time. Waiting to be moved
by the impulses of heaven. To have the chance funnel
descend. Into the grassy bird lit day.
                    And so much talk of the heart
and the breath is nothing if not practiced in this
            helter skelter. In this wondering wound.

So much sorrow winds around me ridiculously. This sweet refuge
of home won't give up, is compounded of hard objects,
            of floating mind, shelter, walls.

                        Tin hearted memories, chemicals.
We fight incredibly through a hideous mish mash of inheritance,
forgiving for deeper stamina. That we go on, the world
            always goes on, breaking us with its changes
until our form, exhausted, runs true.

THE BRAIN IMPRESSED IN ITS ODDITIES

is full of futility. So there.
I'm going to go off again, I know I'm going to
go off again. See, you're all fixed up now. A joint

approach to welcome these days in.
But how on earth do we *live*.
in our houses, internally, out of it, in it, yap
yap. Not that I think all poets should be doing
the same thing, but, sometimes all that can speak
are the eyes, off my Ass!

I'm going to be a poet, I can put it together too.

Life is beset by small accidents.

MORNING MESS

Just waiting to go out there and boogie it up
In case anyone comes by

Everybody practices magic
                whether they know it or not
        Oh I'm worn out
                just watching the cats
            lick their fur
                I'm worn out
                    fading fast
                        my *hair* is arranged
    the boon of illimitable life is obtained

Bright, sparkling
days come on and out
of each other.
I'm going crazy jammed in. Wanting out there.
No miracles will ever
Happen again. I am really into a ready death.
Stoked up on the fuels—what ever happened
to consciousness raising. Pure and simple
people ready to celebrate everyday.
Faced with a thousand
incompleted tasks, I'm ready
to shuck it all. Take me south
of the border down   border down
Mexico way.

SATURDAY FULL MOON SEPTEMBER

I seem to have paid $40 for half a lid of grass,
    maybe Colombian, full of seeds
        which I must plant in order to make any even claim
        to responsible finances

        And the sun has gone behind some hot moving
        dragon clouds
                Now cooler

        the noon whistle goes off

And then, Thursday again

        some night long desperate consolation,
        affirmation, situation
            reassurance of a good time

I'd like to magic you on this grand occasion
    newly out of the shower

        And now I've got to run

        Frozen bamboo in a screen

                Oh I am so happy this morning
                fairly ecstatic
            Thinking of you
        as always
Bo-Bo Blue Skys
            Hey old Fox, I see you
        Slipping away out there
            with the young fir marching down
                our California coastal slopes to dragon Buddha Pacific
    Wow!
            Hey Frog
                        Yuk! Umlaut OM a lot
Let's walk around the yard once, OK?
        Oh sweet, inextricable time
            Silent minutes of 8 Fox Sparrows
        arranged in Coyote Bush
                    people calling to their animals
Oh this is so fun again
            I could sit here forever
                but I must go & cut the grasses
Observing the amenities of the day

To be frank, the sparrows outside have captured my attention
I give up.

to them because they are so delightful. They have even found
how to sit in the bamboo (given to me by Margot Patterson Doss)
            planted four years ago.
        in this very dirt at the corner of the house.
Ho Hum. They are busy popping around. They are finding lots to eat.

This highly agile barbaric now departs to the kitchen
            adios   adios   adios
                    it is peanut butter time
        Seeing magic in all those birds out there
                    I depart   I depart   I depart

There are so many letters I would like to write.
But let them come through, on attentions and thought.

Intention and thoughts of me.

The green dragon of spring
and the white tiger of fall

And white tiger she go out at night and bathe
in moon waves, splashy foam

Lord! I am riveted in attention
of the future, when pad pad pad
          the spirit gets released and growls its courage
          back.

          Caught up in the placid hills
I must away to the scrub bucket right now. Humbly.
So the wash gods will have company.

I am afraid
of the time past. . . . it is gone

                      and I
am searching in this present

to get full. . . . of its reverberations

               Give me a little humble pride to tell
the story

I think I may have to do this forever

                   just forever & ever

SILVER CITY OVERLAY

(for Turkey Buzzard)

The past has vanished
The future being unborn has not come
into existence
And the present cannot be fixed as being
in the present

Timeless Sighs

Whither rideth us, huh? to what timeless
shore shall we float
in our quest, our homely quest for carrion
Come back little heart, I miss you.

Hey big bird, you of the squashed consciousness
Here in soft May Bolinas breeze on the porch
I want to fly overhead too, with the Crows
Suddenly free
And down comes Mr. Blue Jay
into the grasses, You with the most
silver grey chest
and into the loquat fast what's
happening. And suddenly
the sky changes, and earth gets still.

Waking in the night with sinkings of mortality
I am still, alive, this morning. One would do well
to just look, this place where I begin free

each day to take the path.

Up My Coast
Spring 1976
(from C. Hart Merriam)

First, there were the First People
And the First People changed
into trees, plants, rocks, stars, rain, hail and
Animals
and then Animals made Our People.

Light comes from Sun Woman. Whose body
is covered
with shining Abalone Shells.

                        She came across the Pacific
on a raft.
So did Coyote. Sun Woman kept on going.
Come back! Coyote sent some people to get
her back. She wouldn't come back. So
Coyote sent enough men to bring her back
whether she wanted to or not.

                        They tied her in ropes
and brought her back
to make light for her people. She was so bright
it was hard to look at her.

The people began to walk around and find things to eat
                for now they could see

Moon Man, Coyote Man, and Lizard Man made the People.
They argued a lot.
Moon Man gave People his head
but Coyote Man said he should have paws, just like him.

But how can he take *hold* of things
said Lizard Man,

            thankfully winning his point,

                     and gave us
five fingers, just like his own.

                Coyote was pissed
and he's still hunting the lizard.

When the first person died, Lizard Man felt real bad
and set to work to bring him back to life.

        But Meadow Lark came

              and drove him away saying
People no good, People smell.

           When they die, they better stay dead.

———— ⊗⊗⊗ ————

Robin brought the fire. He traveled
a long way to get it,

              and every night on the way back
he lay with his breast on it,

          to keep it warm.
It turned his breast red.

         He gave fire to The People
and put some

      into the Buckeye tree

      so they could get it whenever they needed it.
Just rub

    the Buckeye stick against

             a dry wood stick.

    This makes the flame come out.

    Humming Bird brought the fire too

      just look under his chin.

Coyote was sitting on top of Sonoma Peak
and the earth was all covered with water.
He got there from across the ocean
                on his raft of tules and split sticks.
A feather comes floating up from the west too.
HI! Who are You?
                        And the feather doesn't answer.
        So, Coyote tells him all about his families and friends
        and What's Happening!
                            And the feather leaps up and says
I'm Falcon! Wek-Wek. Your grandson! Wow!
                                So they talk
every day
        and after a while Coyote Man notices Frog Woman
        always just jumping out of hand.
                            But the water
started to go down after four days and it took her longer
        to leap to the water so
                        Coyote Man Caught her.
                                    And
when he caught her, imagine his surprise!
                            She was his own wife!
                from over the ocean! Small world!
Then Coyote Man
                took a bunch of feathers of different kinds
to the top of Sonoma Peak   and Threw them
        into the air
                    and the wind carried them off
        and scattered them around
        and the next day there were people
                        All Over the Land.

Coyote Man brought the *big clam*

                    to make shell money
and planted it at Bodega Bay.

                    This the place
          and the only place
          where the *big clam*

                    was in the beginning.
Where ever else you find it now,

                    the seed came from here.
     The Tomales Bay people

                    got their seed from here.

Meadow Lark Man can be a pain in the ass.

                    He already said people
          couldn't come to life again on the third or fourth day
and he talks too much and gossips

                    and says awful things to the People.
He says, I know what you're up to, you're really stingy
          you're only dark on the outside.

                    Under your skin
          you're as white and mean as a white man.

When People die their ghost crosses the ocean
     over the path of the wind
          to the Village of the Dead. Sometimes
               they come back and dance in the roundhouse
                    You can't see them
                         But you can hear them

THE CRYSTAL IN TAMALPAIS

In Tamalpais is a big crystal. An acquaintance told
me the story. A Miwok was giving his grandfather's medicine
bag to the Lowie Museum in Berkeley. He said this man
took him over the mountain Tamalpais, at a certain time
in the year. I believe it was about the time of the
Winter Solstice, because then the tides are really low.
They stopped and gathered a certain plant on the way over
the mountain. On their way to the Bolinas Beach clam patch,
where there is a big rock way out there.

                                        Go out to
the rock. Take out of the medicine bag the crystal
that matches the crystal in Tamalpais. And
                        if your heart is not true
                        if your heart is not true
when you tap the rock in the clam patch
                                a little piece of it will fly off
                                and strike you in the heart
                        and strike you dead.

And that's the first story I ever heard about Bolinas.

DESTRUCTION

First of all do you remember the way a bear goes through
a cabin when nobody is home? He goes through
the front door. I mean he really goes *through* it. Then
he takes the cupboard off the wall and eats a can of lard.

He eats all the apples, limes, dates, bottled decaffeinated
coffee, and 35 pounds of granola. The asparagus soup cans
fall to the floor. Yum! He chomps up Norwegian crackers
stashed for the winter. And the bouillon, salt, pepper,
paprika, garlic, onions, potatoes.

He rips the Green Tara
poster from the wall. Tries the Coleman Mustard. Spills
the ink, tracks in the flour. Goes up stairs and takes
a shit. Rips open the water bed, eats the incense and
drinks the perfume. Knocks over the Japanese tansu
and the Persian miniature of a man on horseback watching
a woman bathing.

Knocks Shelter, Whole Earth Catalogue,
Planet Drum, Northern Mists, Truck Tracks, and
Women's Sports into the oozing water bed mess.

He goes
down stairs and out the back wall. He keeps on going
for a long way and finds a good cave to sleep it all off.
Luckily he ate the whole medicine cabinet, including stash
of LSD, Peyote, Psilocybin, Amanita, Benzedrine, Valium
and aspirin.

VISIT TO MAYA LAND

FALL 1976
Chiapas

Marian Lopez Calixto's Story

In the time of the ancients
the earth went dark for 5 days
and they broke many pots
   and the pots spoke
And the demons in the dark came forth
      from them:
The lion, the snake, the jaguar
And the people perished from them.

The little children sprouted wings.
   "You will die mother".
And the child went outside
            at once
And changed into a bird
   And the children survived.

At dawn, no single person
      left alive
Only birds,
Jay, woodpecker, sparrow . . .

Then the people were *transformed*. They were good
   again. The sun came out
      in soft white radiance.
            And our father in heaven came down
to make some other people
   First from clay

But they couldn't move well
and he destroyed them again
    Pulverized the clay
and prepared the clay
    and made the clay alive.
And looked for food for them
    But they didn't like the grasses
he gave them
    so he gave them
                the delicious part
    of his thigh.
And they fought trying to take it away
            from each other.
"It must be that they like my body then"
            said our father.
    And the clay
            began to talk
    and became human
one part man, one part woman.

Helloooooooooo

Are you here now?
I am here now.

Are you here?
I am here.

Have you come here?
I have come here.

Will you drink a little
                    to sweep away the fear?

Breathing the gods, getting the goods

I dreamed I went to see the officials
                        of our town
    They were seated at a long table
    I was handed a basket
    Inside the basket were many flutes
I chose one,
            one that was not too new.
I had been given the soul of the flute
                    That is how I can play
                                the flute today

                            Just not too far away, the dreams
                    just on the other side,
            of this lazy after comida dream
                    the Dutch students playing ping pong
            and softly talking on the other side
of the courtyard; Beach Boys from the boys'
    room.

        Now vast sky   of clouds move over
        Now the sun warms
            the land's dreamy Español

my lord
   I, Joanne
      where, am I in time
   Me is memory
through the courtyard door
take me out, take me out

The cross is an entrance   to the other side

Now coming on to six darkens
    a stream of mist dissolves down
Magic Mountain top.

Nancy reading her 12th
    John D. MacDonald mystery in 4 days
reaches for and sips her tequila drink

    The big fat reefer is smoking
me up
& Chick Corea takes me out
    the window to high sky ledge
big deep silver billows

    To be same here, people
from Bo-Bo land
  I know where my loyalties lay
        hey-hey
    See how easy this is, sweet flame
now lights the table.

        What are you going to think of next
that's going to be liberated
    here in Mexico where I am
for *focus*
    and I feel bound down
        7,000 feet up

in this mountain basin
working overtime to *understand*
        hundreds of little worms in the broccoli.

Close to tearing my tears away
away now crystal tones of xylophone
say sky now dark
and our lord passes

under us, has passed
under us behind the magic

mountains of the west, bye-bye
shooting star now falls

Coward! Chicken! false nerve eater
Emotional hungerer!
unconsolable!
Peanut eater!

I come down here to perish
in the same air? Huh?

Alas, goodbye, bug soul
about to be burnt
in busy fire now
fancy transformation
into ash, how fast!
all this happens.

After the flood only one woman is left, with this dog.
And she finally fucks the dog, and they have a baby,
Who is the first Ladino.

Well then . . .
And now
And right now then
Look here
Pay Attention
Get this
Look right here
And get this right now

Lord Jesus Christ

In the holy name of my lord
　　as much as my father, as much as my lord
　　Coming Young, Coming High
　　the flower of your sight
　　the flower of your face
　　is our days

It is for this that I ask pardon
It is for this I ask divine permission
Because perhaps it is an illness, an ending,
　　　　　　a pain.
Where did it come from, where did it start?
　　　　Holy Mother, Holy Father
I reach to speak to you
I reach to move my lips to you
　　with a little incense, with a little smoke
　　with the flowers in 13 bunches
　　with which he is going to bathe his head

I ask divine pardon, permission
　　　　for perhaps it is his perdition, his sin

Now Comes Young, Now Comes High
　　　　the flower of your sight
　　　　the flower of your face

I ask divine pardon, permission
In the flower of your sight, your face
In the place where his heart is content, his house.

In the place where he wakes up, his house.

All Holy Fathers, All Holy Mothers
I reach to your senses, to move your ears

I reach to speak to you, to move my lips to you

Around
Your holy vision, your holy faces
   Holy Fathers, Holy Mothers, My Lord

Have their spirits commenced to return?
Those of our forebears, those of our ancestors

Release their spirits, release their souls

And send them to us

Find your way to come to our house
the humble place of our wealth

Send them to us

to our house
the humble place of our wealth

May your flowery face

shine in soft brilliance
in white radiance

That you may watch over us.

We look at each other together
Our moon, the mother, and I

THE WONDERFUL FOCUS OF YOU

1977

I've had this dream before
                        the continuity

Just like wild radish kingdom drop their seeds
        all over

            Times to sit   with the tidings

February 14

                Tuesday morning on Evergreen

                    Here at home
                in wisps of spider plants

            I cross to the neighbors past February
blues.

            And I know this is my focus to meander

for days around here around the calendulas
                now happily reseeded next to their old roots

Shabby Lady

                You mixing up my time

and changes of who I am and it's all

                    in the teeny trembling world

February 15

Want to go in dream space go
    to sleep while buzz buzz
        over this resting form reforms the information
        of all the days before

            Interior wanderings pass
        all this time
    with Scarlatti's new piano notes that go on
    into time floop, flop, plop
                    into messy plot

        didn't get me out there to strut
    my stuff enough of these hours
    of middle afternoon wandering

February 16

    Bell time

        Who are these nameless men?

    Food. They are food.

            Yeah, off into the raptures

March 1

> At the Bookstore
> What am I going to do
> What ever am I going to do
> I'm going to do this
> And I'm going to do that

March 2

> Green Tara you mysterious adventurer
> reaching under my pillow case
>
> Torn into the charming fertility of dreams
> The awful emptiness of you
> who won't let me come to your heart   Downtown
> I'll go and let the cold
> unfold

March 3

> Some kind of sleeping form some kind
> of bleary beery bated breath
> No more of coming home
>
> Somehow in rhapsody out there
> in the night
> the diamond bracelet makes
> its light

March 15

Hello nice

Moon face   reverie

You aren't the only
part of the mysteries that move
through the airs
as interim in time that moves over
and over again in the day down the street and up
again

March 24

Inside rainy book day

Wish you were here—
My dog has fleas—
My dreams
My dreams
last night
     I'm never going to say
last night again

March 23

I LOVE! today

Way back in the rooms
                    Way   Way   Back

Soy lo que Dios quiere
I am that which God wants

                    The wonderful focus of you

March 25

Echoes of the many corridors

actually they aren't echoes but combine reruns
of what's out there comes back

and boy am I tired

            rains a little, sun comes up
            rains a little more

                    I believe people give
            each other what they want

            Brilliant quince in bloom,
            the wonderful focus of you

Watershed and Cosmos
Still this April 7

I am the Bodhisattva

of this day

Yeah!

April 8

How can I be so awful

April 15

What

a week. Compassion
    hate, hope, illness
        In the thick, on the edge, over the edge
    on the other side, back

on this side again, my friend
    we meet again

April 17

Beauty stands back

                        Dress up for the model

All these little adornments, the earrings
        and beads, hats
and scarfs
           days drift by in the world, day time
           night time, day time, performing

the functions of living
                     I'm asking you
       over, over here wet
     Pacific

Cruising

April 30

      Cats stretched out before $50 worth of propane
  loose, with such surprising subjectivity I must
     have been born before
  to have learned all these thought forms
        itself over and over in delicious little scenarios

     From the North the blue headed wind
   Goddess, remember her with the rest
  of her 6 compatriots
        I mean her six companions the Yoginis
and another six from the West, and six
        from the East and the South too
All imposing and strong and bearing the heads of animals

    The Mighty Goddesses are
          thought forms, are OK
     convulsed with laughter, OH
         is That what you look like OH
  the white rock rose is blooming, AH
      Bhagavan Das tones thru noon and after

May 2

   at 2, Good Lord
      I have been breathing all day
     for which I thank you and yawning
     and arose swimming and sleeping upon the warm waters
      of the ocean on my way to shore
    towards you

May 11

This day blooms auspiciously
in grey

"Something will happen if we let it
Everything happens no matter what we decide"

That
just lets it go, doesn't it. Waiting and
tidying for your arrival.

My Friends, I thank you all
for what accompanies me

My Lord take
me to the voice
and let it float

I will sustain you
the door is always open
Unlimited and Unceasing
like the sky

July 21

        Yesterday the heron covers
the sky in front, that's a good sign
     and hummingbird wants to come in
this morning's back door. Wake up

I'm over Here
         Utmost uproars of emotion

       Owl on the roof
   top, Buddha in the front
seat

More on Thursday

     And then not so much more
         But it's Thursday
    again
    And electric enlightenment is in Pacific
        blue air pelicans dive
     and I'm the kundalini snuggle that moves
            on the mount
      of baby fawn spots
    leap into the crazy arms of the impassionata
utterly consumed.

August 1

Bruised, I am totally bruised full moon
    comes up as the ground rises up
under, stronger than I am, whap whap whap
    and then I die, but I don't Really
die even a small death and I come thru anyway an episode
  of arrival
      Fuck it is this a battle
  war makes on July 31 the summer
of '77   Help!
      Is this heaven or hell or summer camp
where all is well

August 9

    No where but here
  Absolutely accurate aim
in the new sound of rain
        and little whispers in the wind
  are words that say names
No yesterday, today and tomorrow
  Woman looks at Nam
gets big dive bombers from heaven
    This about the time I start to take a shower
and lose two lines
    which may come back
  and this the time when I start
the dinner curry
  with tomatoes
    or not

August 16

Get over it or get under
    One sits and thinks alone
many thoughts
    trailing the whimsical garments
of time
    Great thoughts of him, ahem!
    Say goodbye, release me!

    So I can love again

    What's for lunch
    What's for breakfast
    What's for gut stretch
        Shucks!

Say it brother, I want
    to be free
and walk away
    from your smile and feel
OK after while

September 5

September Monday Labor Day
    Bakery opens
Red Bi Plane in Blue Sky
Does a Dis play for Bolinas
Kent Island Silver Spider
Line in Pine Tree

Go home alone

September 15

> Oh this visage
> of the divine honors
> the very embodiment
> of aristocratic loveliness
> lotus seated
> 'Insensate in a whirlwind of desire'
> The swinging music
> slide guitar
> And now brief September
> sun ends
> after six's rising
> coastal bands of fog

October 11

> Oh well, it's a grey day. I paid all my
> bills. I'm not in debt to anybody
> Little birds rustling but I can't see them
> Huh! what's wrong
> On October 11, 1977, with me this heart
>
> that belongs to body, speech and mind
> tied with a scarlet cord around
> the neck of the high Himalayas
> I'm inventing this emotional
> life of place
> Meanwhile back in young man
> paradise across the street
> everybody wants a car and I'm drinking
> gin in the just about closed out occult mesa
> of dusk new moon
> waiting to be called up in the fire
> of the new season

206

November 5

A preserver, a taker care of
where is my earring wire
and early morning rush of Gato
Barbieri brings great I love you to
this romantic soul, the shower
is running, election day
there *is* no better place

Sink into the great
peacock graced bower

December 20

Warm grey overcast and rushing winds

of morning take me to
the empty space inside of worn out blues

Phooey

Full Pacific Moon

Time is a nice thing to go through

207

And with March a Decade in Bolinas

Just sitting around smoking, drinking and telling stories,
the news, making plans, analyzing, approaching the cessation
of personality, the single personality understands its demise.
Experience of the simultaneity of all human beings on this planet,
alive when you are alive. This seemingly inexhaustible
sophistication of awareness becomes relentless and horrible,
trapped. How am I ever going to learn enough to get out.

The beautiful soft and lingering props of the Pacific here.

> The back door bangs
> So we've made a place to live
> here in the greened out 70's
> > trying to talk in the tremulous
> > morality of the present
> Great Breath, I give you, Great Breath!

JANUARY 23, 1979

You believe this stash of writing is "scholarly"?
Out of this we deduce . . .
From this we can see that . . .

      I know it's a detective story of passions,
dinners, blood stuff around which the history of our lives
crank.
      So enough of that tune I was singing there
further back, I'm up to date with the day-glo goods
of modern historical revelation, barely a day old.
It's the hungry growing of the future who wants to know
if *you* know. So what

about that deer in the backyard eating down the as yet
unborn apples. A little deer go away dance? bang
bang on the pots and pans? when just last summer it was
a heart-stopping glimpse of nature's larger grazer?

You *fence* it in.

A few days later at the washtub
    spritzy subject on the fine high jinks
sum up time, exams
        Caw caw Caw Caw Caw!
      These three black crows have lots of news
    overburdening the other sounds
newly arrived in this location
such as myself five minutes ago
definite need to be reassured
    that the present has always existed.

THE DEPRESSED ENNUI BEFORE 11 A.M.

Now's the time to catch it in words, those pungent
rebuttals of "Hello, I'm just sharing my heart for breakfast now."
And it is time the Goddess of Compassion had her incense lit.

And from her inner lit path, she made her way looking
for her shoe. The dog had taken it.

And now off the top, I present you with seaside memories,
and an adventure to boot.

          The memory part is meandering
along the channel as the tide rushes in
    And the man with the secret life gets swept right along
under the pilings of the houses, and fights back to land on the
      rocks.
      He walks back to the lady on the towel,
      immersed as she is
      in the newest freebox soap opera, she has just become
        aware
      of the danger of the situation. He lies down
      and goes to sleep.

Stripes of red, black, and gold.
So essentially I'm at home today
      trying to get the garter snake
   out of the wash tub
    without picking him up.
        How much time
    can I spend
regaining these refreshing circumferences of the day.

The importance becomes so slight
   with desultory trip downtown and back
A half a peyote button, a little break
    for erotic fantasy; David Hockney, painter
   in New Yorker interview seems very productive
and social at the same time this takes me to my own
    book shelves for a two o'clock cruise of Brautigan
on the top shelf.

        And thence to elmer glue surface
of Robert Duncan being mounted by grand gold lion a la 1958.
And also artist of above, Madam Nemi Frost Hansen, reclining
      on honeymoon,
peeling slightly.

        The news comes in by telephone,
gee, am I far away? Contemplating Larry & Susan's
Fire, and the excitement of ending this day.

Not much time left,
    now for this day's
   entry into type
     a half shot into Baba Berrigan.

I'll check my wiring, get my veins relaxed, recover from the
 reefer
     downtown with M. Rafferty
        just happy I'm here.
    What do you think of me?
      Abalone sheen
        strikes lightly
    Whitey speaks so wisely on the inventiveness
 of human life, excellent blue eyes.
The Dalai Lama in San Francisco yesterday.
       I call Philip Whalen but he's gone
     down to Tassajara Zen Center
    but there's Buddhism in the Air anyway
    with its hesitant Orientalism
   in cultivation. Positive forward proof
 or relocation breath like me interested
in prolonging history.

MY HOW THE DAYS FLY BY IN LIFE TIME

So now the sun shines
        on Raggedy Ann. Light October days
     of confrontation sagas
          and specialties of the heart.

So now the little points of harrowed necessity.
The Poets of Bolinas?
          Hurled against unresisting walls
into the neighbors' lives, therefore living
    in the same house, need these words to fly
past the sink, into the casual flower
    arrangement of the eternal surfaces
        for breathing in life, My life,
which still wonders at the relentless role
        of being born human, once again.

HAIKU FOR CHARLES BERRARD ON HIS 40TH BIRTHDAY

Man get relaxed

Woman get permanent

In my dream last night Deer Lady
                    is dressed in human clothes
Someone wants to make love to her.
She resists
She is lying on her back
He persists
Her four hoofed legs are dangerous
He enters her
She kisses him
                    Her lower jaw
            a deer jaw
Is pronounced

Thursday hot sun dries grasses to gold
                    Looking for the drapery
            to be lifted in preparation
            for the animal bridge, the 'wild' world
of land outside the door

Yesterday when Diana drops me off on Evergreen
and I walk to the cypress hedge entrance
the mother doe and her two fawns are grazing.
                                    Alert
head up, one baby watches as I stop. Wild animals
give off strong ripply vibration auras, like eucalyptus
ready to catch the wind. They groom
each other, color of the dune grasses they stand in.
I am non-movement watcher. Bambi fawn
after eyeing me starts walking in my direction. Wow.
Sharp hooves. He's got his eye on Ita Siamese,
other friendly living creature, sitting
next to me.
                    That's *who* he's interested in.

The Karmapa spoke to me from a center of light
"Your works will flourish"
Let us see his strength and pray
      for his well being.

World needs Lobelia to flash
together in the garden
      Golden Crown
will come to his call
        In the world beyond
Is this world

      Has come and gone
with pair of Osprey
soaring at RCA Beach
      while we light low in the foam
      while we lay low

GOOD MANNERS

The Bodhisattva waits
until everyone is finished
before he excuses himself

Morning is such a welcome time. It doesn't demand
much from the pocket— Some coffee, a cigarette,
and the day starts, full of optimism & clarity of hope
While the Muse holds her head, and the crazy Elementals
        hold down their wrath
lightly under the earth's surface.
                            Some vague attention
            of wind stirs the golden oats
and Ita Siamese drags her breakfast rabbit over
            the roof three
times into the house and escorted out
            the door. While Aram Saroyan & W. S. Merwin
            debate the paucity of their fathers' feelings
in New York Times reviews,
                            the deer
            coming down the pathway still
        are my startled guests as this morning proceeds normally
        out of doors.

Dinner at Briarcomb, that Artists' posh retreat.
In an effort to make the hostess "relaxed" I refuse
utensils and the large damask napkin
and demonstrate how to eat
just with the hands. Quite simple.

Like they do in India!

Her name is Kate.
I sing K-K-K-Katy to her, to put her at ease.

My absolute BEST worst.

THANKSGIVING

On Birch road is a large gathering including Anselm
from the city. We have found a companion for him
who speaks Finnish, since that is his native country.
We are very proud of our thoughtfulness.
She enters the party and we are all expectant.
She speaks to him in Finnish.
He frowns. He looks blank.
They turn away.
Both decide the other is from the C.I.A.

DECEMBER 25

Bill Brown has discussed his Christmas day
dinner for some time.
We drink excellent wine
all afternoon.
The little stuffed game hens
are in the oven.
The afternoon passes
and evening begins. We check the hens.
The oven is not lighted.
We eat them anyhow.
The *wine* is still unblighted.

PHILIP WHALEN'S HAT

I woke up about 2:30 this morning and thought about Philip's
hat.
> It is bright lemon yellow, with a little brim
> all the way around, and a lime green hat band, printed
> with tropical plants.
>> It sits on top
> of his shaved head. It upstages every *thing* & every *body*.
He bought it at Walgreen's himself.
I mean it fortunately wasn't a gift from an admirer.
Otherwise he is dressed in soft blues. And in his hands
a long wooden string of Buddhist Rosary beads, which he keeps
moving. I ask him which mantra he is doing—but he tells me
in *Zen*, you don't have to bother with any of that.
You can just *play* with the beads.

DAY AFTER TED BERRIGAN'S MEMORIAL READING

Out back with Dante looking down his nose, kind of low
      limbed anxiety. Sigh. Don splitting cypress
      from huge pile felled last winter.
                        Is this the form

      I come home to? Yes, and beyond too, oceans
      of paragraphs reiterate the everyday story
      of amazing circumstances in life

                  And now the memory is mine
      of your welcoming encouragement,
          greetings at the door, and that
      'Bolinas looks like Korea'
             certainly an exotic touch
      of patience walking thru the streets. Enough!
            I didn't travel
      to the city for words of you but kept it here pretty

well, your picture and some incense— In due respect I was
      so sad now
            Dante is in captivity
         the night passed peacefully
       gliding up one current and down
thru another city.

January 12, 1984

Hello '84
                              Ted won't
be in this year. Like dropping in.
                                    I want
you and I to be
                special in memory's bright clear bobbing flows
        of paper and time.
                            I dream
of the worn
                obsidian arrowhead found high
        up in lagoon channel cliff side
where the ground used to be.

June 26

For Ted Berrigan

                Unexpected gifts
            that liven the moments
            in our breathing days
                weighs
            heavily on me haunted "not free
            from the memory
        of others"
                    Jogs the evening ceremony for you
        with lightning, thunder & rain, gusts of wind
        brings your card   and our collaboration
            almost a year old.

Monday Afternoon May 14, 1984:

Now we've gotten that out of the way
We still have a ways to go
                          to take us thru the time
of this afternoon's wanderings
                          in the rooms of this house.
                    Two shades of red
matted behind Lynn O'Hare's new painting make it
too busy. The wind

is gusting horribly today. The Pacific Sun's
Lorna Cunkle refers to Bill Berkson's "ramblings
of an agitated mind" in his new book *Start Over*.

                          Gets me pretty anxious
too. Berserk looking dragon from Nepal gives
a frenzied stare across the room, as afternoon light
falls thru it.
                    No birds are out today. Definitely
change Lynn's matting, those reds are chatting up

a storm in the corner. A house is protection today,

against all velocity outside going 50 mph.

And this is a *famous* wind. It's already dangerous
          on 6 o'clock   TV tonight.

Giverny   I am for Gee Verr Nee
                       I see
in purple and gold this time of year
               I am in long   gold   rays and I am in ah
I am in ah . . .
              and I am in Long Gold Rays . . .
                             So Great!
Do you think Tom Clark is really coming to town?
When he comes to town
              You can say
              I see you are coming in
on the Long Gold Rays, the Long Gold Rays . . .

So profound . . .
            I met this Canadian Indian
who said he could bring   the wind   or make
    the breath   of the earth   rise   with attention   Me
Too   said I,   multi crystal medium   thru ruthless talk
    I try to talk   Numero Uno

                                 JULY '84

Itsy Bitsy Polka Dot Review

Well, I'll never *sell* myself
out of whatever I've *got* which is, these days, folks
which is these days, folks
is um
damn hard to come by

Fall Equinox

A lone
hummingbird sits on the limb where there used to be
two
and now the hose is running
water into the garden where once you used to water
the garden too why only yesterday
I saw you outside in the back garden watering some
plants with a watering can.
As I now water
the Iris I mess around with my thoughts
Missing you
in Fall's purple blossoms my sleeve   sniff!   is wet

From PHENOMENOLOGICAL

It is raining.
We have our straw hats
and our clear plastic capes.
We have gone
to the top of the Temple
of Inscriptions and down
to the Tomb of the Great Ruler
Pacal.
I am making a place
in the doorway of the Jaguar
Temple in the jungle.
A river runs below
the foot of this place
and the trees and vines
are deep and lush and green.

Monstera, birds nest fern,
bromeliad, ceiba tree, and an arm
thick vine reflect my attempt
to display them
in the form of this body watching
The Temple behind
my back
The room in which I sit
flashes gold
thru the satiny silver air

And the iridescent blue
Butterfly is folded
up today under umbrella leaf

The room is reflecting
    Looking thru this mind
        Listening, tidying up, seeing
Top rustle of leaves as big snake
Rushes down to the stream
                        in rain time.

Don has walked to the top of the jungle ridge
to a clearing and a little settlement of
Mayans. 'What are *you* doing here?'
'Well, I'm a Botanist.'

        Seated by the side of the Count's
        Temple fourteen toucans
        fly by black in grey sky and

        Black head, white eye band
        Chestnut back, gold chest
            Insect catcher

A real Meditation Temple Garden

As we get ready to board the jitney back
to town five o'clock closing time, an
American camper truck pulls up and a
pleasantly plump white haired lady
jumps out asking excitedly
                'Where are we!
        What's the *name* of this place!'

Morning
Temple of the Cross

The Guardian of the Temple is a Butterfly
we call the Ambassador

        The Ambassador greets us
    sits on my hand
        then Don's where he stays
while Don takes several pictures
    of it on his finger with
        Sun Temple backdrop.
Eats a grain of sugar from sweet bun
    gets its proboscis stuck and goes
        sugar stoned for a while

A wonderful jeweled ornament on the light
straw hat, on the very finger
        that writes this now.

    The continuing embellishment
    of Life in this ancient
    Epitome of grace
        Our eyes are blown up

    Long human calls
    away in the jungle
        repeated over and over dying
    wails, mournful,
elder

And then the Germans
come loudly taking over
    the territory and enter into
the jungle path, their voices
first muted by
the trees make loud sound to cover
        their unfamilarity to
    keep together a noisy
    assertive bevy.

    Then friend butterfly
is back in brown and red and yellow
        the most beautiful guard
    of this Temple.

Self Loathing & Self Pity
I finish Somerset Maugham's biography
on almost empty Wharf Road Beach.
   —terrified, lonely, crazy, no religion, dies
at 92.
      "I think a Tragedy has occurred"
notes Charles Reeves as I give him a ride up Terrace
as we pass Sheriff's vehicles in front of Richard Brautigan's
in front of Richard Brautigan's house. Well he's gone

away, maybe
    a robbery . . .

OCTOBER 25

Tuesday May 7

The wind thru a field of wild oats
How long does a second last

Friday May 10

Nothing. Elm has never looked
emptier or longer, hiking downtown
with 20 pounds of Hearsays

Monday May 13

A long smooth body is yours
as I lay dreaming
He sleeps dreaming beside her dreams
Brown Iris, brown iris
Purple
Lupine on the hills, as green
fades into early summer.

LOVE BOAT

Lynn doesn't want to miss the full moon tonight
As she saw it last night
                As she saw it last night an hour
earlier.
          At 8:30 settled on the Wharf Road Beach
We wait
      in the early dusk
           with a bottle of special
Tequila Lynn has provided for the ceremonious occasion.
"We" are Donaldo, Bill, Lynn, me, & Tom the Eskimo man.
          Earlier we had picked up Tom,
the Eskimo man
         and Donald was surprised to find
      that he wasn't an Eskimo
But an Englishman.
         On the Beach we finally get in the right
seated positions next to each other. Make up
    Haikus about full moon. Bet on
where it will come up: empty beer cans
          against empty
    clam shells
And watch the boat anchored out in the bay
        It seems to be gayly decked with lights.
We fantasize to wile away the minutes to moonrise time,
     sipping the ceremonial tequila
that it is a gambling boat
      with men in white jackets
    and ladies in evening gowns. An elegant
evening of entertainment out *there*
     while we sit straining for moon to rise
over Tamalpais.
   Bill is starting to get impatient.
   I think he is going to hail a Taxi at any moment
  on the empty sand beach

I hear a strangled cry from Lynn
down the beach.
I think she is being sucked up in quick sand.
It's Moon.
Rising up over San Francisco!
Further south than we had ever dreamed.
And Moon is orange, then with a black band across
like a pool ball   or Moon in *mourning* And Moon
has perfect face   Like *Man* in moon
And then Moon's
water touched lights reach across the channel to us
and there is   Moon Head   and Moon Body   and each of us
sits or stands at the *feet* of Moon.
This week
I find out the boat that kept us docked in our places
watching the minutes away to moonrise
was a German freighter
which having unloaded its cargo of coffee in Oakland
was anchored out there a few days waiting
for orders to move
—named TEQUILA MOONSHINE
Light Touched Waters

Yuppy Wittgensteins Arise!

And sleep again the puzzle
  of dream
      Gee glad you've got a horizon
  to speak to You
are as humorous as the hospitality you enjoy
So you must go to the Dentist
         just like all humans do
      so similar to watching the moon
  rise upon its occasions and all our normal
body functions.

AUGUST '85

MIWOK MANDARIN BOLINAS BAMBOO

What's that fur rug hanging over there—
Deer passing thru

Ah it's socked in today boys heavy metal
and soft soft grasses

You know   when you write   poetry   you find
the architecture   of your lineage   your teachers
like Robert Duncan for me   gave me some glue   for the heart
Beats   which gave confidence
                              and competition
            to the   Images   of Perfection

        . . . or as dinner approaches   I become hasty
                do I mean PERFECTION?

                                        SEPTEMBER 17, 1986

"Oh Man is the highest type of animal existing
   or known to have existed
      but differs from other animals
     more in his extraordinary mental
   development than in anatomical
structure . . ."
              Well when I think of men
       I think of them in a sexual manner
Otherwise, I don't notice the difference, you know

being absorbed as *being*   one just thinks 'people'
and not 'male' and 'female' so much as someone
to talk to. And how men are all

the same being born from Man and Woman and out
   of a woman's body commonly known as 'Mother.'

"And God said let us make MAN in our own image,
   after our likeness and let them have dominion."

     And "Nature may stand up
        and say to all the world,
          'This was a MAN!' "

     And then "I pronounce you MAN
   and wife."

      Daddy you is dandy

when you're here. Shrill and soft old Autumnal

    winds blow   and we are tucked below

the shallow soil where seeds spring
                              up and wither quickly
                  flirting madly.

                        I've got him now,

          the beautiful one for my part

of the year here in my dark
                        and expensive underground
          all mine before he is shared

and killed again by the fearless boar
                              he is hunting and torn apart
and his blood runs out and red roses and anemones

bloom   and it is spring   and
                              he is gone again

That man about town gone again . . .

Anything that is *created*
      must sooner or later die.
              Enlightenment is PERMANENT
      because we have not *produced* it
    we have merely *discovered* it.
                     —Chogyam Trungpa
                     Died April 4, 1987

      Many years ago
I am going into San Francisco over Mt. Tamalpais
to read at a big Poetry Reading
given by Chogyam Trungpa in honor of the first visit
            of the Karmapa.
I am very very nervous   I wonder if the car
      will make it
         I think I may die at any moment
When I get to the place of the reading
               it is very gracious
     there is a bar set up back stage
The poets are given a little bottle
      with a hand lettered label
    saying "LONG LIFE PILLS
          FROM HIS HOLINESS KARMAPA"
I am so nervous
I swallow them down right away and feel better *Whew!*
I ask Michael McClure, Aren't you going to take yours?
He says, I'm going to *save* mine.
Years later (still alive) I think of those pills—
They were little seeds
If I'd really done a wise thing
        I would have planted those seeds
         So there would be a whole bunch of seeds

And everyone could have some
                        whenever they wanted them
So now what have I got?   the little bottle
                                of this story—
            and its own Empty Space.

DARRELL GRAY dies when I am in Mexico
I buy and light
   a votive candle in gold-trimmed glass
  for him, light it every night
and blow it out before retiring
     I think of the candle as Darrell.
   During this month-long ceremony
  two tiny moths dive in
  and are enshrined in wax
 It is placed with the Navidad Crèche
 and little by little
 the wax burns up.
      I wash and polish the glass
and it shines
    I think Darrell is now an empty drinking glass
   and leave this devoted attention in Mexico
  for the next hand to fill up.

Tuesday October 27, '87

Finest   first rain
Finest   first rain
           and the black lace mantilla
     the foamy ocean
    the exuberant show off
  General admiration and good will
The man full of diamond light
            —as if many diamonds are shining inside him

      It's never really the same hunger
     is really over-fed accomplishment
    of the hungry ghost asking   Is this really a life,
   a *way*, are you part of HISTORY?

A turquoise blue balloon   caught in the pine
         over the white
       shell beach of Tomales

Look deep and make a grateful show
         over that little silver beach.

FROM THE JATAKA TALES

He   gave the king a charm
                          giving knowledge of all sounds
From that time he understood the voices   —even of ants
But if he gives the charm away   he dies
It is not good to destroy one's self
LIFE is the chief thing
What can man seek higher
And so he listens
To the voice of the ants: So little   is So Big

8 '88

Take it O Moon on the run

Take it O Moon on the run . . .
O moon on the run
    in my back yard over the septic tank I don't
want to pay more taxes.
        I'm not on the money train
choo-choo advancing into financial
maturity ie   Expansion.   The same or *less*

that's fine.   For me.

8 '88

Narcissus

"Credit
I never get any *credit*
　　for what I do—
No one *thanks* me
I do all these things
　　for people
　　　　and I never get any *credit*
I want to be *boss*
I want to be in *charge*
I need money *money*
I never get any credit
People don't thank me
I hate them. I hate this
　　town
I am so lonely. I've never
　　been so *lonely*."

SATURDAY FEBRUARY 4

White sheen on open Bolinas ridge top
powdered white sugar
the whole long ridge
is covered with light   dusting of snow
'this has never happened
                    before in *my* memory . . .'

Dazzling surf clouds snow
And the plum blossoms!

Donald took a picture of it
I tell Arthur Okamura via phone who says
HE has just loaded his camera too

I mean the ridge has been covered with snow before
But not this *much*. And certainly not in one's
own backyard on the mesa   looks like frost

Looks like Alpine Pacific Village Picture Postcard
Actually it's very cold here   and has been
      since December except in the sun.

And the whole shebang, the whole ridge line
            looks like your HAIR Duncan
Gleaming, silver, white. Happy Birthday.

                            for Duncan McNaughton

FEBRUARY 7 TUESDAY

The phoebe in the icy cold wind darts quickly
for food in the air while the flock
of meadowlarks pecking on the ground wander
near the house at the edge
of the meadow. Nothing stays still
for long they are gone.

FEBRUARY 17 FRIDAY

Mist   on the orchids
and Mist   across the ridge   warm
sun at the door   come in

DEATH VALLEY DESERT NOTES

in memory of Harvey Brown

With depressing & unexpected news . . .
Into the new moon
Green rock strewn oak dotted hills
Into Joshua Tree desert
How quick
How grieving
Better by Shoshone
Picking up by Zabriskie Point
One being climbs up inside another
                  for the revolution in art.
                         Signals of old
news on the unexpected desert rock
    A huge explosion
of clarity makes a hole 800 feet deep

And now it's awesomely silent
And there is a Raven Witch
                Where shall we camp

I mean we are walking on an old stone beach
           when we see the horned lizard
And there it is again! the old newspaper rock
And the heat, and the sand dunes
           and the youthful exuberance of the artist's
      palette in green
        russet, yellow red oxides in the hills

So, remembering to chronicle
           events economically
      and learn how to sit

properly were what I thought important
to learn from this space and respect
and awe majestic old time news

SPRING 1989

INCENSE FOR THE BUDDHA

Boy do I burn
a lot   &   that's about All
I do.

OCTOBER 24, 1989

Friday 2:44 P.M.

The sun is about to pass
    from behind the last tree
    in the eucalyptus grove   Soon in a few
more minutes maybe five
                    to spend gazing at the wild ruffle
        of scrofularia, coyote bush, coffee berry
                        Just waiting, & waiting
                to finish and lie down
again while the sun keeps its downward path
                    before drowning off Agate Beach reef.

Chin in hand I see them bobbing along the surf line
    in tender dalliance
Lovely to remember while the westward orb silhouettes
        the sickle shaped leaves of the grove
        and we'll soon be eyeball to light
        soothing the musing of expectation—
It's here   the moment begins.

NOVEMBER *17, 1989*

Haven't I seen you
here before?

That's me!
When I began.

DECEMBER 11, 1989
for Nancy Davis

Cold
Full Moon
Restless
Fill up chattering monkey void with stories
    all night long, visit the Zen Center,
Swim in their pool.   Do I have the lineage?
    When does the transmission come.

DECEMBER 12, 1989

In Memoriam

First, there were the FIRST PEOPLE
And then the First People made the ANIMALS
And then the ANIMALS made Our People

And this is Memorial Day   weekend with unusual
      rainy overcast skies,   tide the lowest
In twenty years causing the Agate Beach parking lot
      to overflow with cars and their human content
      visiting this Ocean withdrawal phenomenon
   much advertised by the media.   Place to go to, Kids.
   All camouflage revealed in air.   You know what I mean—
It's the littoral zone. Where human feet can squish
   the living daylights out of cowering anemone
And the local boys can *walk* to the furthest reef pool
      pick up their abalone and go home.
      So far out, this a view to be seen
      inside the flight of 70 black brants that didn't
want to move,   they *didn't* want to move.

MAY 26, 1990

FROM THE LIFE OF NAROPA

So

he gets fired up and burnt up
he is in great pain

burnt out
nobody's home
nothing doing
okay
keep that vivid vivid   experience
alive

Commitment

'Oh teacher let me give you this bowl of food'
'It's delicious'
'Shall I get you some more?'
'Yes. Go ask for some more.'

So he does, and gets beat up.

No second helpings here.

SEPTEMBER 10 AND 11, 1990

It certainly was divine running into you

Well, just a momentary good idea as your form

changes so often I can't catch

                    up to you *now*
        a large hawk sitting in the loquat tree close

    to the ground and then
      you are thunder growl borrowed from the northern

storms   on their way   in a day or two and leaves
      are bedding their ground around the buckeye

    The little chirruping flocks.

    Kwan Yin Willow

              new moon
    has hardly seemed   to grow.

SEPTEMBER 25, 1990

FRIDAY NIGHT

       In pale blue dusk   sky   Moon
     is nice light gold.   Oh where
   are you going
my favorite friends in a flock   Gold crown
song is going north
   for the summer   has different
  seeds up there   up there friend moon
is getting larger.

                   APRIL 26, 1991

There is a mouse under the sink
Little mouse turds around in the kitchen drawers
It is raining, storming
The refrigerator
has gone to the dump
Donald's back
has brought him to bed for several months
He can't move
The war is skidding to an 'end'
Who wants to kill anything.
Buy two mousetraps
                    and leave them   unset
around in conspicuous places
I think it's gone away.   One day
I take the peanut oil from under the sink
The top is gone.
Inside the peanut oil
is the body of a mouse.
Oh!   too horrible
Look   look at this!
I put it outside the back door
The top of the bottle is really very narrow
He wiggled in head first
He can't back out
He's drowned   but preserved
He's in his oil tomb for two weeks
On Easter day I look at the bottle.
He has risen
            to the top
Donald   now walks

Buries mouse next day.

APRIL 27, 1991

OCEAN PARKWAY GAZING

I

Ocean up
against cliff
   Long thin roll
of surf over

  longest shale reef of the North Coast
and way out tiny point is buoy
   is light at night
   signaling danger
     But this morning is peaceful
     Just light
movement of breeze cool caress
  like a nursery song.
Flat glimmering gliding surface
  Past echium's purple plumes in hues
 spotted with bees
Catching a morning breakfast.

   The Coast Range rises light
    mossy green and in its folds
   dark design
    of fir, redwood and pine.
   Monarchs 'empower' this scene
    when they land
  lightly in their cruise
   for nectar. Poison oak
just a yard away.

   The voice describes the scene
    looks up for reference
     listens to two

263

song sparrows carry out
their call

And response as the hissy light
waves roll over changing continuum.
The minutes go by the sea
The sea closes in
Up to the edge
of mythology.

MARCH 17, 1992

II

Muso Soseki
companion on the bench
beside me
restless surface watching
the minutes, endless
silver inlets
down the coast

8:28 A.M.
March 24, 1992

Specially
For Your Eyes

  If you make it this far you are fairly out of danger
   because now you are on foot
on dirt roads, edged with sunlight
    and small birds. When the wind
comes up you inhale it whole
      and slowly distribute it
     calm the torrent of breathing

MARCH 30, 1992

ADONIS IS OLDER THAN JESUS

Ever heard of a place called Byblus?
An ancient place
with an ancient god
a great god
called   El

and where King Cinyras
father of Adonis
ruled

And Byblus remained
as religious capital
of the country

on a height
beside the sea

And further south
the River Adonis
falls   into   the sea
from its source on Mt Lebanon
a day's journey away

Oh the River Adonis
rushes from a cavern
'at the foot of a mighty amphitheater
of towering cliffs
to plunge in a series of cascades
into the depths of the glen.

The deeper it descends
the ranker and denser grows
the vegetation, which sprouting
from crannies and fissures of rocks

spreads a green veil over the roaring
or murmuring stream
in the tremendous chasm below.'

Freshness of tumbling waters
                purity of mountain air.
An old temple marks the site of the source,
        a fine column of granite, a terrace—
And across the foam and roar of the waterfalls

        Look up
        to the cavern and   the top of the sublime
        precipices above

Seaward when the sun floods this profound gorge
        with golden light
                fantastic buttresses and rounded towers
                of this mountain rampart are revealed

And it is here

Adonis meets Aphrodite for the first
and the last time

And here his mangled body
is buried
And here every year his flower

the red anemone blooms
among the cedars of Lebanon
and his river runs red
to the sea
'fringing the winding shores
of the blue Mediterranean

whenever the wind sets inshore
with a sinuous band of crimson'

Once a year his passing is a cause
for lamentation and commemoration
In March
     when early flowers
          bloom baskets
are filled with earth and planted
   with wheat
and flowers.   Tend the fast growing shoots

    for eight days these gardens of Adonis
      then flung into the sea
with his image
    as sacrifice
  to the new growth of the season

and with songs that the lost one
      will return
   and ascend to heaven
  and ascend into sprouting wheat
    into passionate   life again.

Tender life again.

SPRING 1992
With thanks to Sir James George Frazer

Again   recognizing
the impediment of quirky sadness
Where does it come from?   This shortness
of teary breath—there! it's gone
in a sleepy time funneling of physical emotion.
It's not so bad.   What is it?
                    I hope Dave Haselwood
does not think too badly of my shortness of control
                    on the camping trip.   Can't you just
          let it go, those impediments.   The anxiety
     of packing up 'things'.   We drove over a thousand miles
          on that seven day trip, circumambulated the Siskiyou
Mountains, sacred to Karok, Yurok and Tolowa people.
But abrasiveness in the back of the truck where I lay seeing
     row upon patches of mountains, shaved of trees.
          And look around, where did the money, the wood
go. Don't see it here, didn't stay for long.
          One immobile rabbit as guardian
          for the empty campground
                         Fallen fir giants
in the   forest around.   Mossy rivulets abound
               With great sorrow we had to leave
          the beautiful place,
     we *had* to leave   that beautiful place.

JULY 6, 1993

269

How *Does* one attain that popular narrative
tone so conducive to rendering the   ancients
immediate and palpable?
Pretty intimate   thru illusory   time
and with a lurch of a heart   beat
his hand is on my shoulder
'Save all the good parts'
in a low and throbbing tone
'and the gossip'
the beauty light
in the late afternoon

Conversation with
Allen Ginsberg
April 1994

TOWN HALL READING WITH BEAT POETS

> The enlightened man is one
> with the law of causation
> —Mumon

Ed Sanders onstage telephones William Burroughs
in Lawrence, Kansas, who stayed home 'because
my cats need me'.   I go hear him from the back
of the hall. Then it's near time for me to read.

Leaving I pick up some trash clogging the exit door.
It's my book, GOING ON!   What I'm reading from
tonight, those
    'understated Buddhist influenced miniatures'
       (says the next day's NY Times review)

And it's *my* big dusty footprint on the cover.

MAY 19, 1994

271

WATCHING TV

Ahoy!   Electronic nightmare. . . .
          You don't see many Skunks watching TV
          that is,   if you are watching the tube
          you never get to see Skunk outside strolling
          in the full moon towards the compost. Good Evening.
          He lifts his tail. I'm just strolling, so all is well
          with the smell.

          A topographical enlightenment is swooning
          in the back yard. Look at the sky tonight! View
          the promenade of crisp hedges today. 'The world
          around us is workable'   when the mind
          is unfettered and away from the tube, the screen;
          the eyeball engaged in a back lighted room—mind tomb.

Then full moon Skunk appears   delightful
                    with tiny frightful screams.

                              JUNE 23, 1994

Terrace Roads slumps into the Canyon

Just one access to the Mesa now
    with a night stew of Emerson
  until midnight mist light drizzle
and water laden sky turns into downpour
  over pastures of ghosts
    and morning woods of angels.   Does a place

have its own Memory?   I'm on the river
    and cut off by the flood.   What is free
   from cause and effect?   The poetry song stone
that gives off overtones.   The quest
  is to find those lost vibrating overtones
of the poetry stone.   Along the trail
of your little town, sheltered since your birth,
   the beautiful land.   Intense nostalgia
    invades my soul! Carrying Ita
all last night protecting
  that warm old cat body
   in my arms to get her to a place
of respite, comfort, and safety.

God makes an impenetrable screen
    of pure sky, pulsating
   undulating, casual.

JANUARY 1995

273

I Blinked My Eyes, Looked Up and Everyone Was 25 Years Older—

When you're alive you get to
    recognize hematite,
    azurite, smoked quartz
      lovely eh?
        in sticky black silk

      And watch simplicity
          become complex in management
    'Only bow when bowed to'

    Go look at the sunset
Inspiration for a bunch of numbers
    heralding the close of the Xian calendar
      and new age metaphysical smoothies

Suddenly, I looked up, and everyone had white hair
People go in and out of your life, and your life
is a room filled with flowers and a kitchen cooking supper
and you have wrested the inscrutable from the obvious

or the other way around

We are called the exquisite   bloom of February
We are called wild and grow freely

Very very annoying are people who arrive
an   hour and a half late for lunch.

MARCH 1995

"REPLACEMENT BUDDHAS"

> The altar of Buddha is dark
> The room has been taken
> by the dolls.
>   —Gyodai

What do all those Buddhas *mean*
            at the museum, brought from elsewhere?

Rhetorically, What do these apparitions signify?

"A magician mutters a spell over stones
and pieces of wood and produces the illusion"

of Buddhas and humans and animals and houses
"which although they do not exist in reality

seem to do so." And some people blinded
by this magical hokum-pokum

hanker after what they see— The Buddhas and fast
cars, race horses and glamorous people—

        forgetting they are just stones & bones
        pieces of wood

    Translucent like last night's dream

from The Life of Naropa
MARCH 18, 1995

WAKE UP

Wake up this morning and gingerly open

    to the heart.   What

    does it feel   like   now that Franco   is gone

Yesterday   Duncan knocks   and firmly   closes
    the door   behind him   'Franco

       es nada mas'   Just got

his letter dated seven days ago   the words take on
    sweet   final   meaning

    'I love   to   work

    in the   cool   mornings

and meadows   with   the   whole   Alpine   show

    are   terrific'

Terrific.

    In the   whole   of   space

In the   whole   of Clear   New   Space

    for   you.

AUGUST 27, 1995

276

VIEW NORTH

Back dropped
   blue-grey clouds
    warm lull
  a spot of sun
in this clearing
   of moment transferred—
a perfectly peaceful point
  of view—

Larry Eigner's window.
  Salute you Larry!
    Seagull cries 3 times
  and then the crow,
 also a reef grazer,
slowest, easiest,
   then smooth layers exhale—
Don't let yourself get away
   from that conversational
   tone line of the reef emerging
    low tide, windless

FEBRUARY 2, 1996
In Memory/Larry Eigner

Bob Marley Night Saturday Downtown

Dreamlike   the lights have a dark smoky glow and the street
is filled with groups of people under twenty.   Car radios
groups of boys, groups of girls, three sheriff's cars.
Like spring break at Fort Lauderdale, but here everyone
goes home before morning.

At the Community Center the reggae is authentic, easy and
slow to dance to.   The group, from Mendocino, has served
'jerked' chicken for dinner.   I go around back to see if any
barbecues are still set up.   The plaza is filled with vans,
their own encampment.

I walk up and start a conversation with a man and woman
cooking. Like, Lovely evening, how lucky you can park in our
plaza, which we don't usually allow, don't you love our
Community Center, and that's our freebox over there, etc.
She says, o God

they told me   there would be people like you   here.

MARCH 18, 1996

So, well, now,   You've got it

Alone

behind the scenes with the dishes

and a fast embrace

with Robert Duncan's Hestia.

—I practiced being true

to you and desperately

Angry also just for the force

of that energy as independence

and the foresight that nothing

lasts forever

—PUSH OUT   THE BREATH LINE—

Please no more ad nauseam dinky words
down left hand margin of paper
datedly practiced by second generation
New York School   stuck on their typewriters

SEPTEMBER *1996*

Snapshot for Lew Welch 25 Years Later

Hold on to the bright

Time memories   Bolinas Bay
eases in   with flat
smooth curves

in front of the slope which gradually
falls away through the years

A turkey buzzard
family of three are hunched
atop a bent-over branch. One
raises its wings to the early
morning sun to dry

Directly down-slope behind them
white lacy patterns
of water fill the picture

A while to groom   and wake
to small circles breaking
the surface of the bay down there—
a sure indication
of edible water dwellers

seven surfers cruise the mouth
of the lagoon

Curving antlers of a young
buck rise through the scrub
at the bottom of the gully

A bit of transplanted
pampas grass waves airily

The turkey buzzard
    with wings outstretched is still

a totem.   The deer still
  as it gazes frozen up-slope
   at me penning this down
    for you. Then

  such a beautiful exiting
   white furry rump

          9:11 A.M. Overlook cliff edge
          SATURDAY, OCTOBER *19, 1996*

Dear dear little wrentit with white circle around your eye
    bouncing thru   red berries of   wild honeysuckle
      grey overcast and foggy   damp in the studio
the neighbor keeps his woodchipper   going at a dull
    sickening roar hour after hour.   I do not wish
    him well, pulverizing his Mexican oak mulch.
Try to be *vast* now.   Remember this strand
    of conscious thinking vibrating like a watery
    jewel on the morning's cobweb.   All show, plunk
  it falls, so temporal, this attempt to cliché the moment.
As all falls silent.

DECEMBER 12, 1996

282

You?

Was that you whistling for me, the snake in the shower?
The water doesn't really, in the long run, belong
to any 'one'. The wild man on stage shouting the Prajna
Paramita.   'Poetry is about continuing Poetry'. Look look
    look quickly

MONDAY
MARCH 10, 1997

WIDE MIND

Occupies a wide mind, a wide consciousness,
    front page, editorial page
The winds of spring are cold and keen from the sea
    Can one bring dead people to dinner?
        Constantly opening up those dark arms
        'I'm having a ball
            sleeping with my skeleton'   Allen
        before he dies

A harsh hawk-like call from the cypress hedge entrance
    come out   come out!   I am   I am   never
    been here before   See me? Steller Steller

Jay jaunty blue black

'Do you suppose it's him?'
'I was thinking the same thing.'

        Day after AG's passing
        Sunday
        APRIL 6, 1997

ARTHUR OKAMURA'S PIPUL TREE'S BODHI LEAF

All these sentient questions
   for Ficus Religiosus Indica's dark green shining
     leaf and long drawn tapering tip, trembles and shimmers

with just a suggestion of breath, awareness of air, change
   and motion before the human seated below
     in dark and desperate meditation becomes quote
       'Enlightened'. The tree, a companion in mutual

awareness, a companion in mutual enlightenment,
   equally rooted in being in one place
     in a meditative state with inalienable rights
       —'all things' being interdependent and equal

A *tree* achieves 'Buddhahood'
   2500 years ago reflected now in this ancestor
     leaf compiled of the most complex
       ingredients of creation: Sun
         Cloud and Water,
            Earth, Time, Space, Mind, Universe . . .

     Like any leaf
       from every tree.

MAY *1997*

Arthur's leaf designed for Poetry Flash's
Watershed Environmental Poetry Festival,
Golden Gate Park Bandshell, May 17, 1997

FIRST NATION

Back in   First Nation time, morning of the world time
the sun has yet to arrive, keeping all in a silver keening.

Attack a chore and stay there
     Imports are tossed
         on the compost. This
           is about weeding the unwanted
            and uninvited

plant life out of the ground.
           A very short stop for roots to stay
          It's labor

intensive and not mine, cruising the Sunday paper
filling an empty mind with instantly forgettable
facts of global life.   Hello

did you sleep
well in the New World Swing?

        By the Round House they go inside young men
      with suitcases and punk clothes. Gather their power

      keeping the door closed
    Come out birds, deer
  flicker feather headbands, turkey feather tails,
 shiny abalone buttons. Way-ah
it's always been.

SUNDAY, JULY 20, 1997
After "Big Time"
at Kule Loklo, Pt. Reyes

I thought, I'll make it *so* simple

anyone can get it   understand
            not that it would be beautiful
      or anything like that. Remote   maybe baby talk.

So lost that taut story, the reason to head through
      classic epics   to have structure for understanding
      however 'Western'.

Then with the assumption of Pacific   characters
      became mammals or birds, frogs.

An attitude of listening repose   drifting
      through a cumbia tea-dance with Rhamnus californica

      a bushy partner
and an up-beat early evening towhee

      who's not so wild anymore

OCTOBER 25, 1997

GRATEFUL

After two months in Mexico

and continual rain storms here
        to find this studio

not slurped away by a subpocket
of suction hell. Anyway

notebooks a bit damp
and mold has taken
        the last of the faded blue atticus

butterfly. Still *dry* framed
picture of pensive youngster—

'Nobody loves me
I'm going into the garden
to eat worms.'

And looking fairly immaculate—

Trungpa's 'First thought
                Best thought'
        which makes it seem   easy

 'Yesterday I ate two smooth ones
  And one wooly one.'

FEBRUARY 11, 1998

STUPIDLY INSPIRED

It's true

the cricket ate the lace curtain of the studio,   not
relegating itself merely to the hearth, escorted
out the door rapidly in a teacup. There. You'll like it
better in the great wild world of woodchips and ferns.

Bad Vibes a mere drape
for the deeper expositions of life and words. Something
meaningful about existence,   awareness of enlightenment
in a lifetime. Get it while you're alive, can't find it when

you're dead. The simple timeless 'it's all right' satori, no
no-no, that's right, you got it right, believe it.

MARCH 21, 1998

FOR THE PITTOSPORUM TENUIFOLIUM OUTSIDE THE STUDIO WINDOW

Much too hard to understand all
these words about words
beyond words

'respectful, considerate, sympathetic'

Alas poor seedling you have gotten
out of hand, too tall, now
you are almost a tree
and must be 'removed'

A pampered euphemism for 'killed'
for you take away my sun
you are out of place, you were careless

Your seed volunteered itself.   Goodbye.

We both become 'liberated', unattached
to your form
and become congenial

if not congratulatory
at our mutual trembling
in the attentive noon breeze

SUNDAY, JULY 26, 1998

It's So

It's so hot and sleepy at two this afternoon
    and sad too like a skeleton bracing itself
        Do you think some stray word

Will electrify this mess or does one just
    give in to the empty space of the afternoon
        O go to the beach drag yourself to the shore

OCTOBER 20, 1998

NAROPA APPROACHES HIS TEACHER
INSTRUCTION TIME AGAIN

How's it going boss?

Tilopa says Come over here
and presses a burning stick into his flesh. Yikes
this hurts!

Don't you remember this from before?

No limits to the knowable and the merriment
of the Gods and Goddesses over the ignorant
rebirth of the wayward human
which in the long run is really really painful

Here, I'll kiss it and make it better.

JANUARY 18, 1999

TRY

very hard. See
it wasn't so hard
but soft and warm to chase
the dream get worn out
give up again hold this vision
into a heavenly shield
against fear   a 'wondrous
creativity'
against the bewildered
daytime   mind find
teachings in many realms.

APRIL 12, 1999

The 'English' sparrows in the courtyard don't know
    it's the first February of the 21st century

                The lady we buy
our rebozos and blankets from kisses
    the money we give her and crosses herself before
    she puts it in her purse

                The Basilica for the Virgin
of Health is entirely empty for a moment
It's *people* who bring the religion

                                Pátzcuaro
                                FEBRUARY 1, 2000

What you really don't want is some

    overwhelming sadness that says 'Yes
      this is the way it always is'   in a longer   or briefer
sojourn of yourself

            face the face of the innocent Niño
      always seated in his chair
      with the sweet exuberance of youthfulness
      blessing your petition

    Hello to that being

  who buzzes an easy gossip refrain
One of the beloved little angels
    who inhabits the hummingbird
      and brings comforting laughter
        to the darker corners of the room . . .

MAY 22, 2000

YOUR HEART IS FINE

Your heart is fine feeling the widest
possible empathy for the day and its inhabitants

    Thanks for looking at the wind
in the top of the eucalyptus
dancing like somebody you know
well   'I am here   I am here   I am here'

The wind picks up
    a rush of trees waving
wildly for your understanding
—apple, plum, bamboo
        rooted and flourishing
next to your home
in the mutual air
awake without defect

JULY 17, 2000

To Live in This World Again

You must hide yourself
    change your flamboyance
        to a dull hue

DOES THIS MEAN I'LL NEVER HAVE ANY FUN?

No one will notice you
    The gods won't drag you off
        the earth for their own

Entertainment. You are camouflaged
    with simplicity

JULY 24, 2000

I Can't Help It

Wandering through the rooms
Pay Attention   to time
The mortal voice nags . . .

What Happened to You?

Come my songs
keep your face to the sun
and the swift darting swallows

So you can rise far

above this morning's
mundane laundry

In a precious garden awaken
to the familiar cascades
of water
from a grouchy stone jaguar

The branch of a pepper tree bobs
recalls the breath
of Denise Levertov
repeating these words   in Mexico's
eager morning life

Swaying pine tops
in a peerless blue sky

There you are again

Awakening. The pure three note

song   really listening

Look   I'll do it for you once more

To WAY   wheet wheet

Pátzcuaro
FEBRUARY 7–12, 2001

"WHATEVER IT TAKES"

I don't 'get' ideas
if they're too abstract
what's the use
if there isn't action . . .

        There aren't any backrooms out *here* anyway
    in which to make deals
unless they're over the septic tank
        but believe you me people are just as shifty

over their septic tanks as they are   anywhere else

But I was taught self-criticism   as ballast for false
    economic optimism

    "With the relentless harvesting
            of our natural resources
We'll see the downfall of US   capitalism
    by the end of the 20th

        century" said AJ Muste "when we run out"

        Didn't foresee
        the horror of free
        global trade
    terrorizing   innocent patches of mahogany   hillsides

        —the tyranny of the shareholder
        is foremost—

    So far from the Tao
    planes need to spy
        to check the profit margin

Oh do me a favor
and don't rile me

or we'll have a fight before dinner.
and all I'll get
is a half eaten apple
in a brown paper bag

—the Way of Dark Virtue—

The less you know   the better
because 'ideas' can fuck you up

So love that distant cool mind   of practice
in the garden
where seeds   hopefully   are still free
to sprout

and pull out that tiny pine tree
before it falls on your house.

APRIL 18, 2001

THE DHARANI

Hail!   Bear in Mind,   Bear in Mind
the Jewel,   remove disaster, remove disaster
cleanse us,   clean us up,   illuminate us,
enlighten us   Absolutely you can do it

JULY 24, 2001
No sun all day

FOREVER AND A WHILE

There's not just a single actor
  in this story
    We know ahead

Of Time it's already
Happened and will again

While the living
  heart beats

with its pensive security

See these brave creations
  of ourselves
    so flamboyant and deep

In the ponderous reality
  of a real dream's dream

AUGUST 1, 2001

The Fog is halfway over the mesa

My table of life for the past
thirty years or so is not broken
up into incidents as much as continuum

So much for the skill of living
the outer life of season
while the 'inner' buttress
certainly becomes no wiser

Have you heard this a thousand times before
from anybody & everybody

And that's it? Except you allow
the rapid combine of elements
heretofore disparate: like Bodhidharma cruising
the Pacific as a   surfboarding Coyote
and the poor bonged-on-head disciple Naropa
here to meet him
along with the classic
Greco-Roman education
that always hauls Odysseus along
—probably the oldest of the lot

but none of it 'indigenous' to here except
through conviction of the poet   combining

these strands into a useful cord,   a thread

to throw into the dream and see it
come up clear
as a picture in the evening

AUGUST 3, 2001

BIBLIOGRAPHY

The Tapestry and The Web. San Francisco: Four Seasons Foundation, 1965. Edition of 1,000 copies, of which 27 are numbered and signed by the poet and specially bound. 61 pages.

Joanne. Bolinas, Calif.: Angel Hair Books, 1970. 300 copies. 78 pages.

Places to Go. Santa Barbara, Calif., and Ann Arbor, Mich.: Black Sparrow Press, 1970. Limited edition of 750 copies in paper wrappers; 200 hardcover copies numbered and signed by the poet; 26 lettered presentation copies handbound in boards by Earle Gray and signed by the poet. 93 pages.

Lettre de Paris / Joanne Kyger, Larry Fagin. Published: [S.1.]: Botanists of the Rue Vercingétorix, 1976, and Berkeley, Calif.: Poltroon Press, c. 1977. 8 pages.

Desecheo Notebook. Berkeley, Calif.: Arif Press, 1971. Limited edition of 500 copies printed by Wesley Tanner at Cranium Press. 37 pages.

Trip Out and Fall Back. With drawings by Gordon Ball. Berkeley, Calif.: Arif Press, 1974. 17 pages.

Truck: Tracks, Poems by Joanne Kyger and Franco Beltrametti. Bolinas, Calif.: Mesa Press, 1974. 10 pages.

All This Every Day. Berkeley, Calif.: Big Sky, 1975. 91 pages.

The Wonderful Focus of You. Calais, Vt.: Z Press, 1980. 66 pages. Limited edition of 776 copies, of which 26 are lettered A–Z and signed by the poet.

The Japan and India Journals: 1960–1964. Cover collage by Ken Botto. Bolinas, Calif.: Tombouctou, 1981. 280 pages.

Mexico Blondé. Illustrations by Donald Guravich. Bolinas, Calif.: Evergreen Press, 1981. 30 copies. 24 pages.

Up My Coast. Adapted from the stories of C. Hart Merriam. Illustrations by Inez Storer. Point Reyes Station, Calif.: Floating Island Publications, 1981. (First published in *Floating Island II* by Floating Island Publications, 1977.) Edition of 500 copies printed at the West Coast Print Center, Berkeley, Calif. 12 pages.

Going On: Selected Poems 1958–1980. New York: E. P. Dutton, 1983. 85 pages.

The Dharma Committee. Bolinas, Calif.: Smithereens Press, 1986. 12 pages.

Man/Women. With Michael Rothenberg. Illustrations by Nancy Davis. Pacifica, Calif.: Big Bridge Press, 1988.

Phenomenological. Institute of Further Studies. Illustrations by Donald Guravich. Canton, N.Y.: Glover Publishing, 1989. 30 pages.

Book for Sensei: Poems. Illustrations by Nancy Davis. Pacifica, Calif.: Big Bridge Press, 1990. 16 pages. Edition of 100 copies, of which 26 are hand-colored, lettered A–Z, and signed by the artist and the poets.

Just Space: Poems 1979–1990. Illustrations by Arthur Okamura. Santa Barbara, Calif., and Ann Arbor, Mich.: Black Sparrow Press, 1991. Printed by Graham Mackintosh and Edwards Brothers, Inc. Published in wrappers and a hardcover trade edition; 125 numbered hardcover copies signed by the poet; 26 signed lettered copies handbound in boards by Earle Gray; 11 special hardcover copies signed by the poet, each with an original drawing by Arthur Okamura. 145 pages.

The New Censorship. With art by Donald Guravich. Denver, Colo.: The Next Savage State Publishing Group, 1994. 21 pages.

Some Sketches from the Life of Helena Petrovna Blavatsky. Boulder, Colo.: Rodent Press, 1996. 22 pages.

Pátzcuaro. San Francisco: Blue Millennium, 1999. 29 pages.

Some Life. Sausalito, Calif.: The Post Apollo Press, 2000. 34 pages.

Strange Big Moon. The Japan and India Journals: 1960–1964. Berkeley, Calif.: North Atlantic Press, 2000. 281 pages.

Again. Albuquerque, N.M.: La Alameda Press, 2001. 173 pages.

Sirene Nella Nebbia, Poems by Joanne Kyger. Translated by Rita Degli Esposti. Loiano, Italy: Porto Dei Santi Productions, 2001. Edition of 108 copies, numbered and signed by the poet. 56 pages.

A native Californian, Joanne Kyger became part of the San Francisco poetry world in 1957 when she left Santa Barbara, where she had attended both high school and the University of California. After spending four years in Kyoto, she returned in 1964 to San Francisco, where her first book was published. Further travels took her to Europe and New York City before she settled on the coast north of San Francisco. She travels as much as possible to Mexico.

Printed in the United States
by Baker & Taylor Publisher Services